PEACE THE ELUSIVE

RESTS ON TURTLE'S BACKS TO RIDE

DO NOT HOLD YOUR BREATH

By Laurie Hutchinson Zimmerman

This volume is dedicated to my dear second mother, Shirley Mather, with whom I shared many of these poems as they came fresh from the hot oven of my mind/spirit and who told me so many times that I should publish them.

This one's for you, Shirley.

Please, know this from the beginning. These are not truly "my" poems. I shy away from owning them, stepping back to distance myself from prideful ruminations. They come to me from "out of the blue," you might say, the deep cerulean blue, the angry red/orange flame, the healing green of crowded forests, and ask me to take them and make them into what they want to become. I see them written on pages in pencil, held in my hand, yet still, they are not mine. Now, it may seem that I am disowning my children so I can't be blamed for their behavior, but the child shouts, "Look at me-e-e-e!" as I swing through the lines, so there appears to be a small bit of ego – ownership - that wants them to be seen and read.

This is a stone soup/stew into which everything, but the kitchen sink, has been thrown, in strange, random juxtaposition. There will be poems that you love or absolutely loathe, like okra, or cilantro or dill pickles, but everything is in here. I am only doing this once, and it's for me and my family and friends for whom it matters. This is a kind of memoir that, by writing it, has taught me about myself and will open the doors of my personhood to all who enter and read. There is joy, sorrow, self-chastisement, philosophy and contemplation. A real soap opera, without the commercials, the endless infidelities or cliff-hangers and resurrections. However, it is hoped that, somewhere in all the words, there is redemption. With this book, I invite you to join me on my journey.

Laurie

Biography

As a child, when people would ask Laurie Hutchinson Zimmerman what she wanted to be when she grew up, she would, invariably answer, "I want to be a movie star." She noticed that most people either laughed condescendingly or smiled with a knowing, patronizing tilt of the head. Still, undeterred, she attended Stephens College in Columbia, Missouri finishing with a BFA in Theatre Arts. Thereafter, the pursuit of a theatre career was her focus for the next several years. As with many childhood dreams, fulfillment is often detoured, then derailed and often is gently left behind with regrets but with acquiescence to the understanding that life will take twists and turns which can bring fulfillment of different sorts – see the acknowledgement page.

There always was a quiet undercurrent of the writer's spirit, showing up initially in writing songs. The first glimmerings of the poetic spirit came in the form of showers of haikus, hundreds of them, falling on her head, which she called "canapes" and which led her to the "meals" that appear in this volume, with a few choice canapes interspersed, one of which is the title of this book. The creative seed within, which fostered the planting of herself in theatre, took root in the literary soil of poetry. All hail to the written word.

Laurie lives and loves with her husband, Fred, in Hendersonville, NC with their two captivating cats. There are three deeply-loved grown children, two grandsons and one more on the way as of this writing. Laurie is a Baha'i of 60 years. It is this grounding that generates much of her writing.

Table of Contents

Table of Contents

A tip of the hat and big hugs to All

There are so many acknowledgements that are intangible, like the natural wonders and horrors, the erupting emotions, and the random thoughts that spark the urge to write, but there are people who have been the inspiration for most of what I have written as well as my dearest supporters. Among these precious beings in my life are my husband, Fred Zimmerman, my/our children, Ariel Penning, Arrow Zoe Rojas and Jamie Zimmerman and my ancestors for whom I have so much gratitude simply for being part of the wonders of generational life My only surviving first family member, my sister, Lynn Reynolds. Grandchildren, Matthew and Zachery, who have no idea how much it means to have them in my life. Linda Prichard, Linda Havens, dearest sister-friends, have cheered me on before and during the compilation of this book. In-laws, especially, Meg Reed, are on the "squad" of well-wishers, as well. I am ever grateful for the help from Karl Moeller in publishing this work. I also wish to acknowledge the multiples of glitches besetting my organizing and putting it together. All of them taught me something valuable and led me to truly making it come together better and better. Good glitches, all. Deeply frustrating but life is like that, isn't it?

There are two other artists for whom I have special and deep gratitude. Camilla Calnan (Camiphoto.com) who lives and works in the Asheville area of North Carolina covering territory north to West Virginia, west across Tennessee and south to Georgia and who graciously contributed her photograph of the wonderful turtle, who I have named Tallulah, that graces the front cover of this book. Special hugs to our dear friend, Janice Appel, who created the little Tallulah who stalwartly travels through the book to remind us to move slowly, on steady legs, with perseverance on our way to the Goal of Goals.

A special tip of the hat to Linda Prichard, who, today as I write this page, coined a phrase that I may use often from now on: "Gratitude is like butter on hot toast." Melts your heart, eh?

Say Again?

Say again?
What did you say?
I couldn't hear you, water's running.
You like my poem?
          Oh,   thank you.
What?   What was that?
          You think I should publish it?
                    Hmmm . . .
So nice of you to say that.
Wait a minute.
Let me dry my hands.
Come here, you.
Let me give you a hug.

Oh, Those Poems!

They push themselves into my mind up from my heart,
        insisting themselves through my fingers
                to find their place on paper.
And I oblige.
No creator, just a channel.
No determined musings, just discovery.
No ownership, just allowance.
And so, it is, dear friend, that they found their way to you.
I delight in being your server today.
This tray I carry is all for you.
                                        November 19, 2011

BIRTH DAY: Begin the dance

I am crowning on this, my birth day.
My sacred darkness turns to Light.
Ears emerging now.
I know those voices tumbling around me, all filled with
        joy, relief, celebration, no longer muffled by
                uterine swaddling, but sharp and surprising to
                        my new senses.
Little body turns, and shoulders slip into the
        element of air.
I gasp as its chill awakens autonomic instincts.
Breath of Life,
Life of Breath fills my tiny lungs, so ready for this planet.
I am perfect in this moment.
I gush, safely, into Papa's cradling arms.
Urgency surrounds us. . .a cloth quickly wrapped around
        my slippery, floppy body, rubbing, drying, warming.

I am still my mother-self, not yet my other self,
        until that snip that severs me, once and for all,
            from my primal lifeline.
I am placed on a trembling, laughing, crying earth.
She whispers to me, "Welcome to the world,
        my sweet child."
Face-to-face we meet, Mama and me,
And I know what home means.

November 5 & 19, 2013

Time Will Take Its Own

Time will take its own.
No rushing, no hushing, the tick of its passage,
        the tock of its inevitability.
Resign to its undammable flow.
Be the leaf upon its surface.
Be the duck, the water on its back, let it roll off yours.
Be in it.
Be of it.
Though it is illusion, it is what it is.

November 24, 2013

Introduction

I am light.
I am dark.
I am featherweight.
I am rock heavy.
I am hard.
I am harsh.
Steep and deep,
Icy and molten.
Filled to overflowing, empty, vacuumous.
Bound to earth.
Soaring, released to the sun.
I am dancing riotous joy.
I am blanketed black grief.
I sing the golden-throated airs.
I play the crashing metal cymbals.
Embraceable, untouchable, fraught with angst,
      at peace with faith.
Riding rolling waves, drowning in tsunami surges,
      I am more and also less.
I am Life.
Meet me as I am.

November 10, 2011

Life Sharing

I'm here for you now.
I'll not leave you behind, as I stroke ahead in these
     churning waters.
Time may come, you may overtake me,
     may need to gather my pieces.

January 1, 2012

Live Now Deeply

Mark my words.
Mark this moment.
Inhale its timeliness.
Exhale it remains.
Know its temporosness as I extemporize.
It drifts like mists upon my breath, my words,
     necessary as nutrients, intangible as faith.
It ticks away our lives.

November 26, 2013

and the beat goes on . . .

Ever leaping into dawning future, leaving past behind
      in dusty swirls, breaking speed records . . .
Mile a minute? Million miles a millisecond!
Smashing through mirror mirages that show me
      not what will transpire, only what happens now.
Misgivings born of mistaken steps may be too
      troublesome, too time-consuming, too painful to
      revisit in this rumbling, romping, riotous
      route on the rapids we call
"Life on this Planet."
      November 30, 2013

I am Alive in this Creation

O in.
CO2 out.
Nutrifying, purifying.
My body knows its job.
Eyes blink, no need to think.
Diaphragm rise and fall, no need to call.
Pumping, surging, beating blood traversing body in fractal
      mathematics to extremities and back.
The circle of life guaranteed.
Autonomic Nervous System.
What divine delineation! What deft delegation!
Digestion from top to bottom, mouth and teeth and tongue,
      esophagus to tum to colons small and large.
AMAZING!

Transmutation of food well-savored! Full filling!
Complex simplicity.
Governance divine.
Of all essentualities, I am astounded, dumfounded,
        atomically grateful in this wondrous work.
Well, bless my soul, I am alive in this creation!
All the rest is UP TO ME!
Choices tickle, prickle, poke and prod, challenge me to
        pick what's "right," to be bright.
Oh, to have an Autonomic Nexus System
        to make all run so smoothly.
On trust, on faith, on impulse or abandon,
        the dies are cast and draw my journey's route.
Destiny unknown.
I shudder to grasp this power-lessness in my small hands.
But choose I must.
I do.
I will, and know the consequences.
The map is drawn through the eye of the needle.
The mind/body burden of the soul transcribes the saga,
        puts brush to canvas to relate my terminal work
                of art upon the earth.
Interminable imprint upon the cosmic scenario,
AMAZING!
I am alive in this creation.
Its density surrounds with palpable energy.
Absorbed.
Consumed.
Devoured, feeding me on all counts, without question,
        without request, without demands.
I sup with Angels and Devils and hope to know the
        differences.

To wend my way and seed my land, it is my promise.
It is my duty.
It is my honor.
I tend to step forward 'til what is arises
        to face me squarely and roundly trounce me, or not.
If I know the innards on which I rely, I will arise
        gasping?   victorious?
Hmmmmmm . . .
O in.
CO2 out.

August 22-28, 2011

Ink-lination

A fluke? a happenstance? a proclivity? a desire? a fate?
        to be a producer of poetry, a reception station?
They tap my shoulder, tug at my sleeve and, with guns to
        my hand, make me write them down!
Irresistible.
'Tis my hand that writes, my ears that hear them
        tiptoe/gallop through the halls of my home.
But they are not my poems.
I do not possess their language, their cogency,
        but am possessed by them.
When they are placed on paper, I am surprised by them,
        not by me.
And so it is.
I remain, doors ajar, open for visits.

May 20, 2014

China gibbon song

Cosmic message   life prevails

Let the mountains ring

Spirit Speak

I am here to know my now.
I am here to fill this moment.
I am here to charge this space with my Oms, to be
      present in this time, precisely here now, right here,
         left in time, neither room for past nor future,
            to hear the sounds that never have been,
               and never will be again.
See the light that shines just for this instant.
Know the thump-beat heart of existence,
      the stomach growl that tells of your hunger.
Feel the smooth, cool breeze,
      the air mixed today just for you to breathe.
Sense its unique, nuanced scents, savor its taste.
Feel the smile form on your face,
      opening to speak the words that come to heart.
Note them as they touch your tongue and lips to float into
      ether.
Recognize their truth as Spirit Speak, authentic,
      heart-woven, humble, kind, full of grace and
         gratitude.
Utterly peace filled.

                    May 20, 2012

ZELDY: On the celebration of her life
and passing

Zeldy-Jenny-Jo.
Caller of shots--- magnet, heart, hub.
Don't-give-me-guff, sit down it's dinner.
Partner-Pillar.
Mother-Mentor.
Soul Support.
Dynamic Spirit.
Never give up.
Present even when gone.

The Secret of Giving (for Daniel and Joshua)

A little advice: it's nice to share; it's nice to give.
But learn and live.
Don't give it all away at once.
Save some for another day.
Another may await your open hand.
And, my sweet and sharing friends,
     please, set a bit aside, for you may find,
       and no one will mind,
          it's OK to save some just for you.
            At the Reimers, August 12, 2013

Growth

This my body, this my living being, urged to fill
      spirit lungs to capacity, to inhale, not Earth baubles,
         not world matter, but Kingdom wisdom.
May it guide my path with brilliant, subtle light and,
      daily, feed me with true soul food to generate
         unbounded, exuding generosity.
Spiral energy up and out, a kundalini image made
      manifest, marvelous, miraculous.
Such aspiration threatens to burst this self from too much
      want, and take me from this realm to realms
         unknown.
Yet surety of gravity grounds this, my body, this, my living
      being, too pragmatic to take such radical leaps of
         faith.
I remain, retain my fragile person-hood,
      ever open to possibilities.
December 4, 2013

Coeur-Ordinance

When all is said and done, when we hold each other close
      against the time when we must part,
         we dive into each other's hearts, through eyes,
         wide open.
We take up residence, to claim the soil, to till the fields,
      tenderly, for lifetimes of cultivation.
February 6, 2015

Portage

Canoe on too-shallow river, bottom to bottom scraping.
My thoughts – heavy, burdensome.
If I toss them overboard will that keep our boat afloat?
I see I am mistaken.
Take the paddle.
I'll step out.
I'll walk along the shore.
Ah, still too weighty is our load.
We portage then.
It is a task best suited to two.
Can you feel the weight of this vessel encumbers us still?
Canoe, belongings test our strength too much?
Do we agree it's time to put it all to rest beside the water?
To walk away, hands free to hold only each other?
Or open, to receive gifts awaiting us ahead?
Yes?
Yes.

April 8, 2012

Mango Moment

The solitary twinkle-fairy dew drop catches my eye
        this still morning.
Its sparkle is unaccompanied in the crescent
        mango leaves of this great tree, today.
So prolific in past seasons, now almost bare of promise.
Of the dozen that filled the yard a score of years ago,
        she's always stood tall and wide and proud,
                the premiere producer of the fruitful family.
In December, the others bloomed.
Now slipping into May, they hold multiples of drooping
        stems bearing heavy, hearty Hadens evolving
                into great, sweet deliciousness.
Even the small, bent "Grandma" tree, with hollow trunk,
        sharing her space with an ever-enlarging parasitic
                palm, holds all the progeny her frame can bear.
Yet, our queen of quantity showed no flowers 'til March.
Now she expends her energy on new leaves.
So curiously out of sync with her sisters, she resonates
        with my own disconnect as if, standing closest to
                my bedroom window, her inner circulation
                        flows in empathy with mine.
She lives. She is strong.
New leaves from rusty red to fine spring green raise my
        spirit, make me wise, teach me well that flowering
                and fulfillment of purpose need not be –
                        will not ever be – in true synchrony.
I now know that Age and Sage rhyme for a reason.
                                April 29, 2012

Awakening

I am, right here, left here in this moment, this present,
this gift.
No past, no memories, no guilt.
No future, no plans, no anxiety.
I listen to bird songs, rustling of leaves, water flowing in
the pond beneath my window.
And downstairs, the sounds of cooking, cutlery clinking,
coffee brewing, rich, brown smell.
Rise and fall of abdominal breath captures this
hot promise of pleasingly bitter awakening.
Hammer strikes, someone's awake and working.
My body resting, still, in wrapped repose, a chrysalis
opening, responding to these insistent calls
with trembling, arching stretches.
Reveries move me further into now, to that which is,
not was...not will be...just here, now.

May 5, 2012

Now here no where else

Life resides in this moment

Here now or no where

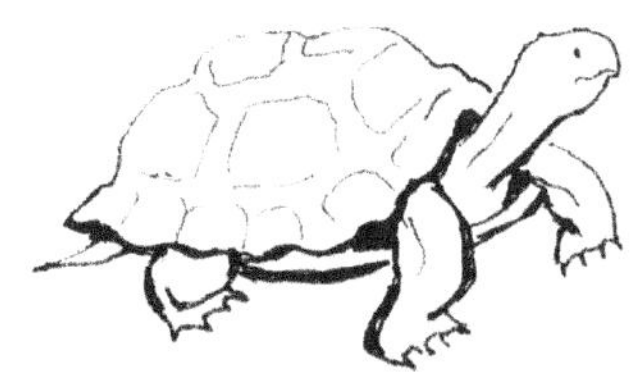

Yes, It Was

I find myself traipsing through the blades of feelings.
In this field of memories, some are sharp, serrated,
     slashing me anew.
Others, smooth and pliable, yield beneath bare feet.
A strange, regressive journey I have no desire to retrace.
Yet, a word, a phrase, an aroma, a quality of light
     compels me to the recesses of life gone by.
No way to alter incidents, accidents, stumblings.
All are woven tightly into the self that is me.
It could as easily be thee. And, yes, it is WE.
It is the fabric of US intertwined with threads of THEM.
ME   THUS   WE.
Letters of the alphabet of humanity, form strands, braids,
    ropes, cables of cosmic communion,
       mingled memories, smacking of past life experience,
        present life participation,
         future fear manifestation.
Streams of Consciousness on which to float like fallen
    leaves, always downstream, meeting at the Delta,
      the mouth which speaks our names as we pass
        into the ever-symbolic Ocean.
Molecular melding.   Brilliant conception.
Calm, tumultuous, maelstromic, pacific, blue, green, dark,
    sparkling source of all LIFE.
H2O,
Home to Organisms, always ready to receive remains.
                 May 13, 2012

It's Time

Time urges me to COMPRESS it.
Go there.   Be there.   Move on.
Go to it!   Do it!   Get it done.
Squeeze, to dry, its life, love, laughter, - its liquid essence.
Soul says, "Hear me!"
Expand -------- Absorb ---------Fill yourself to dripping.
Be the sponge of all that flows, grateful receptor of
        each instant's bounty.
Balloon with untold beauty and
        squeeze yourself out over all, generously,
                never doubting your endlessness.
                                August 8, 2012

Water

I am water, I am mighty.
I am water, I am balm.
I am water, hear my roar.
On the shore, I beat my rhythm, gifting sand and shells
        and lost watches.
I am water, may I soothe your brow?
I will quench your thirst.
I am water.   I am you.
Now watch me etching canyons deeply, rolling boulders,
        trees, homes, steeply.
I am water   I am power.

I blast clean the faces of great mountains.
Be like me.
I seep and trickle to travel underground.
I dissolve elements into myself.
Be like me.
I am water.
Speak kindly to me and I form wondrous crystals.
Call me stupid and there will be no beauty within.
I am water, essential to life.
Be like me and know no boundaries.

August 12, 2012

Jump

Jump with me into this space.
Know its boundlessness, its brightness.
It was, it is, it always will be fresh and new.
Inhale its purity.
Sip its cool serenity.
Turn its creamy sweetness upon your tongue.
Dance like kittens, soar in silence like owls and
      jump again with joy, in this space, with me, my love.

September 16, 2012

Solstice

Let ME go.
Turn M upon its head when double-you becomes
    the norm, and WE prevails.
It's the logic of living, a consequence of giving up
    the one for the joy of two, the thrill of three,
        the form of four, the fireworks of five,
           the marvel of more, - embraced.
We are the ocean.
We are the drops; we are the crystals that arise when
    LOVE is the WORD.
We are the resonance of source exponentiality
    if we only knew.

                    December 21, 2013

At first a Lump

At first a lump of damp clay, gestational forming,
    birthing, emergence upon this earth,
        the kiln that makes our spirits useful,
          the heat at times unbearable.
Re-emergence . . .cooling . . .strengthening.
Glazing - hotter still - 'til, at last, a vessel for great service

                    February 18, 2012

Just Bloom

Just bloom into the moment.
Don't put off expansion 'til then.
BE   IN   YOUR   LIFE   NOW.
Past is passed, future a millisecond away.
NOW IS WHERE IT HAPPENS
Pack it to the brim and overflow.
      Filling Willing
      Living Giving
      Trust we Must
      Abundance to Redundance
      Constant every Instant
      Flowing all Glowing
      Sources Recourse to our need.
An orgy of rhyming reminders to awake, regenerate,
      and leave no room for doubt.

Together

Touch me with your kind hand.
May I feel its warmth.
Look into my eyes, unveiled.
May I know you.
Walk with me, true.
May our strides synchronize.
Talk with me.
May we speak in harmony.

October 8, 2012

Salvation

Release the hounds of guilt that growl and snap
    at heels and heart.
Let go the ghosts of grief and watch their smokey
    wisps waft heavenward.
Fold fingers round felicity and taste its fruity flavor.
Savor the golden moments of grace and calm.
Clarity of vision, surety of sense, tranquility of trust,
    blessed balm.

September 26, 2012

May God be with you

**In those cupped hands find
your home**

Place of Peace Love Calm

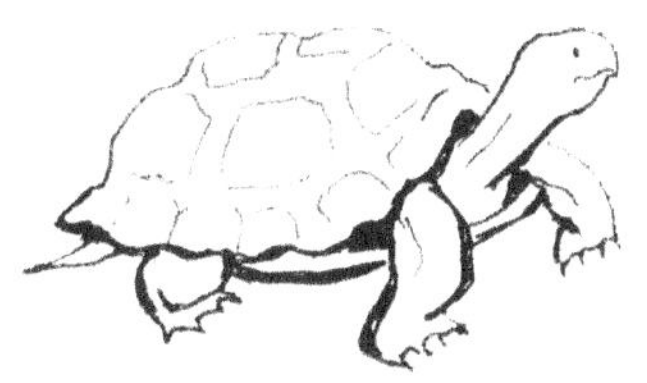

23

A Moving Tale: a poetic journey

Dismantlement, dismemberment, stripping walls,
    laying bare the hidden places, our home
        weeps at our loss.
My soul's home churns with severance.
Removed now, memory only marks our journey of lives,
    soul investments to make sanctuary, labors lavished
        formed sweet spaces within those walls,
            up and down the stairs we built
                to raise bodies and souls within.
The love, the laughter, the trials, the tears, all designed to
    grow us, to make us strong and wise . . . perhaps.
Now, re-assembling chunks and boulders, bits and pieces,
    parts of life unmade - a puzzlement of how they fit
        in this distant space, in this ordinary, cozy,
            cottage, unclaimed, as yet, as ours.
I ponder what was and wonder what will be.
Among these boxes, upon boxes, that fill the tiny rooms,
    I suspect there is, regrettably, too much of "us"
        toted to our new lodging.
Each box, opened, is a touchstone of the past.
Re-touching brings flashes of memor-images, and
    I am delighted to re-find familiarity and comfort
        in these items.
I am here with this inevitable process,
    "settling in" - "arranging."
It will transpire. I will be patient. We're here together.
And that is what matters, anywhere.

April 6-25, 2013

A Snail's Pace

Here am I now in this tiny slit of time,
     this moment of creation, of sense, of action,
        the only moment of truly living.
The snail leaves its line of silvery slime,
     glistening, beautiful.
So each life's journey is marked.
I do not turn 'round, retrace my steps, erase my trail,
     change my story.
Doing so wastes my life time, draws a backward loop,
     a telling mark of regret.
I cannot see this from where I am.
The record of my trek is only seen from above.
Only One sees clearly, beginning to end, the tell-tale trail,
     the forward tracks, marked with too many arching,
        aching loops.
Now awake to this mis-take, this snail, this frail me,
     moves forward.

                      August 1, 2013

For Life

Swans mate for life, and I am yours, too, for life,
     and ever after because I plan to love you, fully and
        more deeply, with each passing day.
With all I want for you, this is what I pledge to you,
     "In life, to life, for life, my love."

Not a Poem

I stand within my being to gather threads of history
    that have no words attached, back to a time
        too early to enjoy conscious contemplation.
All that sponged, absorbed, accepted, unquestioned,
    untested, simply digested as what is true of me.
Reception, conception, welded within that structure that
    forms my foundation.
Now, at 68, my mind-heart-spirit stretches to wrap 'round
    amorphous images to weave tangibility from
        elusive tendrils, to discard irrelevance, and
        embrace what is true.
In this recent residence, so unlike my early years of
    Illinois flat-lands, I look out my windows upon
        forest and hills through screens bearing
        stink bugs, grasshoppers,
        Daddy Long-legs.
They surprise me with their numbers.
Fresh from Florida flat-lands, from which we came
    not half a year ago, I think that fleet anoles would
        have grown fat on these bugs.
And who am I today, with all these years under my belt,
    that I would need to search within
        when there is so much without?
I have yet to find my footing in these rises and falls of
    Appalachian topography.
Unsteady, off-balance, I seek my center for comfort,
    for confidence, but its silence
        is a barrier to my probing.
It comes and goes now in these mountains . . .
The homesickness.
It carries me to re-collections, sounds, images, feelings.

Can I lay them on the table to piece together this
        puzzle that is mine to solve?

I mine the ore that is mine to find, to smelt into
        pure ingots that reward me with their brilliance.
I dig to discover hidden truths, crack and crush
        misconceptions, and blow away their dust.
Yes, this is tortuous, this tunneling.
It is hard work   painful   but it makes me strong.
It gives me the self-essence that I seek.
It is worth it.
To know my core, my center, my soul,
        Yes, oh yes, it is my quest.

September 30, 2013

I am a Baha'i

This faith . . .that wraps itself 'round me to comfort
        and warm my body.
This faith . . .that finds me when I am lost.
This faith . . .that sets me up and keeps me standing
        when I have fallen.
This faith . . . that brings me to tears, but sometimes,
        oh so briefly, takes me to the heights of joy.
This faith . . . that strikes a chord so deep that I become
        symphonic.
This faith . . .the flint that strikes my mind, my heart,
        my soul into flames, a conflagration of response.
This faith . . that grows my heart to embrace all that can be
        embraced upon the face of earth.
This faith . . .that is my mentor, my sanctuary.
This Faith.

October 2, 2013

Peace is . . . a Haiku Renga

Peace the Elusive
Rests on turtles backs to ride
Do not hold your breath

Be alert for peace
Know these pieces of true peace
The peace connections

Peace is deep breathing
Full-filling lungs deep easement
Treasure chest of calm

Peace is eyes to eyes
Recognition point
You are I - I you

Peace is heart to heart
Ethnic embrace color merge
Mutual Respect

Peace is hand to hand
Breaching walls too long standing
Arrive side by side

Peace is fresh babies
Cornucopian vision
See their sweet tumblings

Peace is kids' giggles
Pebble rippling in water
Pure innocence floats

Peace is blown bubbles
Wiggling transparent in air
Known only through sight

Peace is jumping rope
Knowing both sides of its swing
Never tripping joy

Peace is rocking chairs
Back and forth in synchrony
Unified content

Peace is running free
Tireless limbs wide out-stretching
Moving ecstasy

Peace is open doors
Aromas sweet from within
Warm breezes without

Peace is window lights
Guiding the weary travelers
Welcome to our home

Peace is hot coffee
Waking mouth throat heart and tum
The bitter pleasure

Peace is harmonics
Sound blending tonality
Balanced vibration

Peace is how it is
Buried deep by human hands
Exhume its body

Peace is close at hand
Rub shoulders begin exchange
Known through osmosis

Peace is this moment
Living full to explosion
Endless expansion

Peace is not unknown
In micro-moments given
Realized in time

Peace is on its way
Prepare for its arrival
Settle your disputes

Peace is pieces bound
Puzzle finally fitting
Panoramic view

The GREAT PEACE takes time
The GREAT PEACE takes us to work
PEACE promise fulfilled

Clear Channel

I am given all I need. All I need is to receive,
    filling me to overflowing share this wealth
        where e'er I'm going.
Bubbling broth of rhyming vapors wafting wisps
    set down on papers.
I cannot curb this channeled river first the given then the
      giver.
These rhyming rhythms scamper through me
    must write them down for all to see.
Dear reader, this posy is for you.
Sniff its scents, enjoy the view.
                November 16, 2011

Grace of Reason

Gales of trials, breezes of bounties, thorns of roses,
    underbellies of porcupines, blessings of beasts,
      deceptions of divines.
Let me know their place, their purpose.
And, with eyes wide open, embrace the grace of reason,
    the balance that defines all experience.
Transparency of layers, choreography of players,
    weaving, melding tastes and textures fitting
      seamlessly.
Providence.
                June 18, 2012

Grace will fill this place

A heavenly state of peace

May I live life here

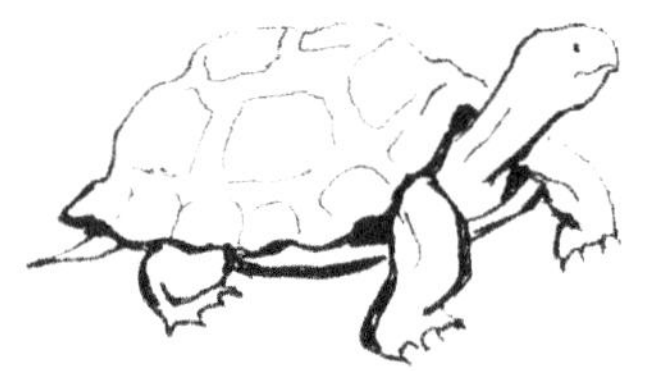

What's Left?

No! No! No!
It's not right!
It's not right!
It's ....Left.
Left in a heap in the corner of the room.
This body, mind, spirit fails to bend to vortexing
        challenges.
It is stiff and brittle, crumbling and collapsing in the
        storm.
I take my meditation, a good, strong dose,
        not transcendental, inside mental, moment of ME.
Slip into the silence.
Gulp quarts of quietude.
Chew upon the tangible textures, savoring release.
Atoms cease rampage.
Molecules dull relentless raging.
Cells find the elusive still spot.
Peace prevails, and I discover a deep-veined,
        golden lode of strength within me.
It's all right.
It's all right.
I am left in contemplative calm to
        renew forward motion.

May 18, 19, 20, 2013

In Rapture

Leaving mind behind upon the ground, with socks
     removed, I feel the grass, the sand, the
         cool mountain stream on my soles.
It's nothing but senses, tingling with elemental intensity:
     air, fresh-washed with summer rains,
     stirs the hairs on these bare arms,
     the scent of green, olfactory delights of
     pine and dirt and earthen mulch,
     a breeze in rustling trees,
     as leaves caress each other.
Bird calls and sacred responses cheer up my spirit
     and the taste of clarity is mine from
         my cupped-hand challis.
Fritillary flyers, caught in spots of sun, capture me in their
     dance and I long to join them.
I am earthbound being now and that is fine.
My time will come, anon.

2014

Untitled: Two by fours

Take no time that is not yours.
Give no love that is not true.
Take no step that is not sure.
Sing no song that is not you.

I am breath.
I am flow.
I am intangible.
I am life.
May 7, 2013

Silence is Not

Silence is Not . . .
Here now I hear naught but the sound of my own ears.
I sense distant machinery.
Shanti dog beside me, sloppy, long tongue
      flapping along floppy belly.
Breathe in golden light, taste bitter rue.
Spit it out.
Relish sweet remedies, basking now in clarity.
The cloudlessness of letting go.

May 13, 2013

Because I Can

Because I can, I write these words.
Because I can, I breathe deeply the fresh mountain air.
Because I can, I hug all those who let me – ALL.
Because I can, I smile and joke and laugh
      and let them know our kinship.
Because I can, I share these brief moments of
      presence and perfection.
Because they can, they let me.

June 4, 2015

Crumbs

I stop in mid-stride . . .
Something is missing . . .
I spin to look behind me.
Yes, sure as sweat on a sunny summer day, there is,
        following my steps, a trail of crumbs fallen softly,
            mostly unnoticed, from a me, formerly firm,
                moist, mindful,
                    now, visibly diminishing.
Walk with me.
I will need your help.
                            November 6, 2014

I Love You

I love you from before time, to beyond our lives, with a
        depth and a breadth that cannot be
            fathomed or measured.
May your heart and soul always know me and
        my love for you.

Letting Go

A melancholic blanket drenched with sorrow and guilt
    wraps around me.
But why?
I am she who shrouds herself in its dark stink.
I, the one who allows it to remain.
I choose its incumbrance, and I am the only one who can
    let it drop to the ground, with impunity,
        to walk away, to begin the journey into
           true self where lasting love and joy
              reside beside recollective reveries.
Rambling through brambles of memories,
    tangled and entwined, I find this mind enmeshed in
      complex circuitry.
Webs capturing dried leaves, snatching, catching
    broken bits of living gone by.

Now become the anthropologist.
Examine these bits of history, these artifacts.
They made their marks.
They took their tolls.
They formed the greater Find.
They can be left behind, now.
No need to scrutinize further.
I am what I seek, the I of pre-birth, the I of post-life,
    the I of eternal purity.
It is not a useless quest, not just mine.
It is Yours and Theirs and Ours, to come full circle to the
    beginning of no beginning, the end of no end.

A shroud is meant to mark the terminus,
          not dragged along the journey.
I think it's time to drop my heavy burden.
I need none of what it holds in its folds.
Yes, I step lightly into the Light.
And You are at my side.
Let's go.

June 12, 2015

*A reminder: Life is a rollercoaster. Where there are "downs", there
are always "ups" to make balance and bestow grace.
But wait, there's more, as they say.

The foot tracks mark treks

On the way back we find trails

Where we might have gone

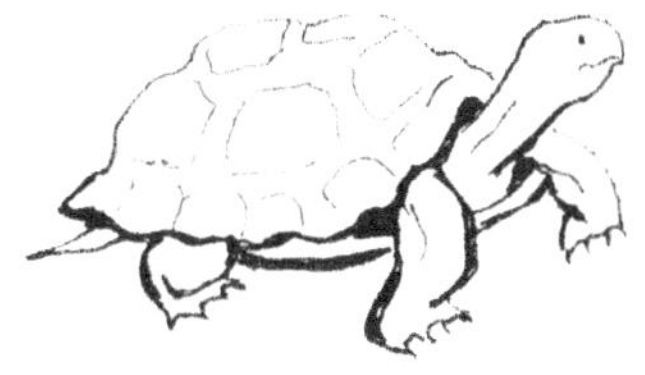

New Conception

Fear   Distaste   Alienation
Isolation   Contamination.
Antibacterial soap and wipes.
Masks and gloves.
Protect Protect Protect.
Security Security Security.
Don't look, it's disgusting.
Don't touch, it's icky.
Don't taste, it's poisonous.
Don't think about it.
We'll tell you what it is.
Here, take this.   Put it over your head.
Stretch it all the way to the balls of your feet.
We know it's tight, a little confining but it's good for you.
It'll keep you safe.
There!
Welcome to the
CONDOM Nation!

August 9, 2011

Words

Words.
Useful ------------ misleading.
Uplifting ----------- daggers.
Overused -------------- under thought.
Chatter ------------ wisdom.
Words.
Commitment ----------- I do.
Denial -------------- I did not.
Passion -------------- I love you.
Passion ------------ I hate you.
Just words ----------- blah-blah-blah.
JUST words ------------ not guilty.
Constant cacophony of letters linked in lines
       straight ------ circular ------ glib ------ pithy.

                     November 8, 2012

God Willing

Oh God, help me.
My God, help me.
My Beloved, help me to fulfill my heart's desire.
Bring me Joy in my heart, peace in my soul,
      gratitude in all my days.
May I not just sing Thy praise but become a resonance of
      Thy grace.
Help me to rise above myself, to speak the Truth
      that all who hear can embrace.
If it be Thy Will, I will.

                     July 28, 2015

Blooming Letters

Your letters are in bloom.
You've sent the fragrance of your love in every word.
I inhale and your scent fills my nostrils.
I touch the page and feel your smooth skin.
I speak your sentences aloud, and your voice echoes in the
      deep and empty caverns of my being.
I turn the pages and there you stand;
      in the vastness of expression you are a present reality.
You are a gift of love upon the page.
You pour it out.
I drink it up.

November 21, 2015

Guilt Showers

Guilt falling in crispy little pieces.
Ashes of incinerated moments past.
Where are the soothing drops of forgiveness and compassion
      that I would pour upon others?
Why not upon myself?

March 18, 2016

Capricorn, the Mountain Climber

Parked halfway between grief and relief to reconcile
     what seems in denial, prospects ahead lie hidden in
        impenetrable fog.
Weatherman says, "Cloudy with no chance of gain."
Meanwhile we tread the choppy waters,
     to keep our heads above it all.
Oh to be upbeat, not beat up!
Looking around, we see humanity and sanity trumped
     by inhumanity and insanity, a maelstrom of mix-up,
        a headlong hurtling race to the darkest of
          bottoms.
I do not root for Apocalypse, but from this perspective,
     it seems to fill the horizon.
Much pain, much suffering.
Such challenges!
We must strengthen to meet them and survive.
Stress makes strength.
Falls teach us to arise anew.
Mistakes take us to better know the terrain on which we
     travel. We are climbers.
The strong, the tenacious, the determined will
     reach the summit to catch the first glimpse of
        sunrise and glorious promise.
May I maintain my footing.
May I find my way to that peak.

                    February 26, 2016

They: The Troublesome People's Alphabet

They are arrogant, they are bullies, they are callous.
They are despicable, they are eviscerating, fatuous, greedy.
They are horrid, they are insensitive, they are jaundiced.
They are killers, they are lechers.
They are malicious, numb and odious.
They are punishing, they are quarrelsome.
They are ruinous, slimy torturers.
They are underhanded, they are villainous, they are   WE
X_________, Y__________,Z____________,
Fill in the blanks.

July 2011

These Children

These children, all children of God, created with the same
     divine intention.
They are not their bodies nor behaviors, but the essence of
     Pure Life in bloom.
They are gifts, blessings, challenges to raise up, to be
     kept safe, to be guided lovingly.
When they are full grown, we will know
     the fruits of our labors.

March 8, 2016

And When I Die

And when I die, lay me down by the mountain stream
      to hear its bubbling waters.
Wet my face with its clear coolness to wash my sins away.
May I leave this life at the edge of purity and join the
      liberated souls, they who stepped beyond before me,
      and await reunion in that Kingdom.

June 19, 2016

Gracie Face

She's draped across my chest, to throat and jaw.
My larynx protests, carotids beat the rhythm of me,
      noticeably.
Her thunderous, furry purring vibrates my brain.
She's got my attention.
Her fifteen pounds tell me of her greatness and confirm the
      richness of our connection.
I endure this invasion of my personal space because
      it's all part of a mutual adoration.
The head bumps that evolve into head-to-head caresses,
      the head twist that becomes almost exorcistic when I
      say, "I love you," the determination to take over
      my yoga mat when I diligently strive for
      asana centering, all touch my deepest
      existential senses and spirit.
When she first came to us with her little sister, Stella,
      (half her size and full of furry affection), a friend said,
      "Speak to her soul."

Really?! Why? Okay, why not? Ahhhh, it is a magic spell.
It teaches me its wonderous bounty and expands to all
humans, animals, trees - even bugs - a cohesive clue
to my quest for humble harmony
and promised peace.

December 16, 2020

Jamie, on a visit to the Asheville hills

He writes.
Poetic passion, turns of phrase, spin into vivid images.
He writes.

He plays.
Long fingers caress guitar neck fretting harmonics,
strumming heart strings.
He plays.

He sings.
Surprising voice, subtle vibrato, reverb nerve pulse.
He sings.

Cosmic collision, collusion of creative juices
blend to bend our ears.

December 18, 2013

What Matters

There now, here now, peaceful, warm, calm delight in
        son proximity.
Brief visit. Present. Gift.
Touch of kinship, expanding relationship.
Celebrate deeply, integrate evolution of spirits.
Sense this precious moment, taste its sweetness.
Savor for remembrance.
Luxuriate in wealth of no denomination.
This . . . this is how we know what matters.

December 15, 2013

The Impossible Dream

Birdsong so pure and clear, I can almost see it split the sky
        to reveal the nether clouds of the unknown future.
That flash of inspiration obligates me to fuse its pieces
        together, on this page, to bring its fragile existence to
                tangible cohesiveness, this intangible dream of
                        Divine beauty, so fleeting, to validation.
It is a task I take on willingly.
It touches my mind, my spirit, with the promise of
        endless possibilities.
With spirit untethered, may I walk, wide-eyed and
        wondering, amongst these clouds of roseate rain.

September 11, 2020

Simply This

Let me know the fresh breezes of open doors, the light of
      unshuttered windows, the comfort of my love's chest
        where I lay my troubled head.
May the sweet and simple things bring my deepest security.
No opiates on the patio to turn the stars into fireballs and
      moths into monsters.
In the evening, the scent of lilacs and fresh mown grass
      suits me just fine.
The sun on my face and the touch of your voice
      become my soothing wine.
Simply this.   Simply this.

June 10, 2016

Heart full of grateful

Feel the grace of this moment

Know there's room for more.

Distance of Time

Time and distance...
The distance of time, separates us from some,
        disturbs the threads of early connections.
Some break, and we are lost to each other for earth time.
Some, so tenacious, hold strong, reunion ever possible.
Deeply woven family fabric can burst into flames,
        spontaneous combustion ending in ashes.
Serendipitous encounters can mesh into unbreakable bonds.
We never know; why assume we do, and imagine that
        permanence is possible?

July 9, 2016

Dormancy

This my chrysalis state, this my numb and slumbering
        existence, this time before time, perched immobile in
            silent anticipation, incipient emergence into
                Glorious Flight.

September 9, 2016

Not the Time

It is not a time to mourn but a time to be born into
        new life-flowing, new knowing, from love lost, death,
            a disappointment, a moment of cosmic change.
Embrace the power within to meet the challenge with a face
        wet with tears of grief and glory, strength, courage
            and laughter in the battering winds.

November 30, 2016

All That is Me is You

I am … I am … I am NOTHING.
I have … I have … I have NOTHING.
In my emptiness, may I step aside from self,
     become a sponge to absorb
          Your Wholeness, Your Completeness,
            Your Volume, Your Love.
                Your Compassion, Your Abundance.
Then, may I squeeze myself dry to drench those around me
     with that which is ALL YOU.

November 1, 2016

Clearings

Clear my heart to perceive,
My mind to retrieve.
Clear my heart to receive,
My mind to conceive.

Simply a Touch

Touch me with your right hand of Love.
Touch me with your left hand of Mercy.
Hold me with your arms of Compassion.
Sing to me the songs of Joy.
Lift me up on the winds of Felicity.
I am yours.
Teach me.

August 30, 2022

Strife Life they do rhyme

The path of least resistance

Cool steps on hot coals

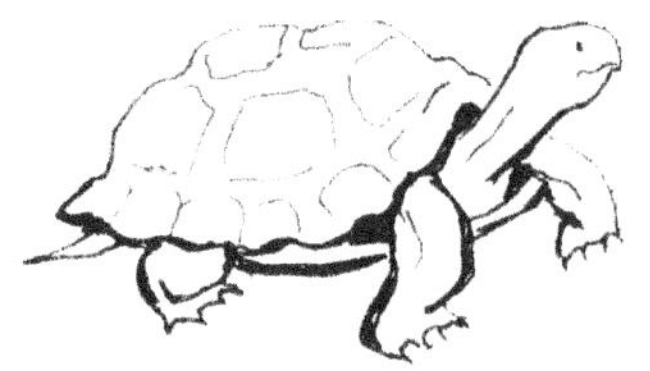

In Mourning

Mourning - its power its depth.
It is the consolation of having loved.
It is the curse of having missed the point of loving,
     that love is the awakening, the stretch of soul sight,
        of heart hearing.
It is taste and touch acuity, unconstrained compassion,
     self-severance, informing the bond of WE,
        unencumbered, without prejudice.
It is the point, the pinnacle, where all ascensions meet,
     the place of ultimate Communion of soul mergence.
That LOVE, that LOVE, that LOVE.
That LOSS, that LOSS, that LOSS.
The Blessed Mourning.

                              February 1, 2017

Infinity...or Musings upon an
empty grocery bag

Now may I dive into a profundity of emptiness where
     there is nothing to touch, and nothing can touch me.
May I feel its wonder, the endless oneness and infinite space.
Let me know the aloneness that frightens and comforts and
     allows my deepest contemplation of Self and All.
Give me time enough to wallow and stretch and vibrate in
     free association with powerful insight.
Let me swim unrestrained, and emerge drenched and sated,
     with no fear, with all great potential to fulfill and
        be fulfilled by promises that will not be broken.
I am willing to dare this impenetrable vastness to come
     home to myself as Me and We. Let it be.

                                  July 4, 2017

Reflecting on our Times

Harvey, Irma, plain common names, humble, unassuming.
We are forced to honor their magnitude, their might,
    their devasting earth nature and monumental
        magnificence.
So, too, earthquakes and volcanos of demolishing splendor.
But the nature of humankind, neither kind, nor humane,
    in its despicable, despiseable dividing of Us and Them,
        rises above natural disasters in its catastrophic
            damage.
Isolate/demonize, on lines along which loathing lies.
Hate/fear, as if there really is difference.
Floods, fires, hurricanes, climate "confusion" poignantly
    reflect the soul destruction of the inner canker
        eating human hearts.

Time now to allot the straws to sip this lot of bitter bile or
    sweet remorse.

September 26, 2017

This poem was written before Maria decimated the shores of Puerto Rico and unleashed the floods of dismissive arrogance from those who should have been on the front lines of repair and recovery. We have yet to know how deep the cancer can dig and how broadly it can spread. It is a long and treacherous fall from grace.

P.S. Maria did come ashore on 9-16-17, but very little was known about its total destruction and unfeeling responses when this poem was being written.

In retrospect, five years later, we look back to see, that our world has become even more deeply and widely divided-between Us and Them.

Kith and Kin

This family of mine, (but is it yours? - sometimes lines blur)
    they're like puppies and kittens that, you know,
        everybody loves. They're precious.
They open hearts and make us smile and giggle and
    laugh out loud.
They cause great surges of sharing where we recognize our
    bottom lines.
They create within our souls a resistance to the injustices of
    arrogant bullies who think they are above humanity.
You know them, the ones who think wealth gives them
    license to talk over the rest of us, we who try so hard to
        express our simple needs.
The connection, the recognition of our commonality,
    gives us sagacity and courage to rise above them,
        to laugh in their fat faces, to walk straight to
            them and OPENLY speak our TRUTH.
We are the wave of the OCEAN of UNITY.
We are the drops who, together, can wash the slate clean and
    start over again.

                        August 11, 2013

For this next poem, I invite you to do some research. It focuses on two
poets, Sylvia Plath and Anne Sexton, who chose their tragic destinies,
both committing suicide. I wanted to contemplate what might have
been Anne Sexton's choice had she not met Sylvia Plath.

What If?

Anne Sexton.
What if she never met Sylvia Plath?
What if the knowing had not given permission?
What if, on the fateful day of that deadly decision to wrap
         herself in her mother's mink coat
               and sit in her running car to end her life,
                    the car had run out of gas?
What if, instead of then refueling to finalize the act, or
         determine another lethal choice, she stepped out,
               removing the remnants of the fatal family,
                    finding a truth from the dead rodents,
                         to rise above hate and history,
                              sorrow and stigma?
What if she rejoined the child that once she was,
         in innocence, curiosity and a touch of delight?
Might she have written no more of darkness and demise
         but written, instead, of release and resurrection?
Might we have learned of the profound resilience of soul?
                              November 8, 2017

Dear God

Make my eyes to see, my ears to hear, my mouth to speak
    Thy Praise.
Make my arms to embrace life with love,
    my legs to carry me forward in Thy Path.
Make my skin to feel the touch and warmth of humanity,
    my nose to smell the fragrance of Words from Thy Pen.
Cause my mind, my heart and soul to awaken to the joy and
    gratitude of knowing Thy Name.
Guide me at all times to fulfill Your purpose for me.
For all these blessings, at all times,
    I give You my self to radiate Thy Beauty.

Spring

Drawn by need and want for warmth and light, I turn my
    face skyward and find them.
Filled with my quest for quiet and peace,
    I turn my gaze inward, and find myself
        filled with grace and gratitude.
In knowing my presence in this space in space,
    I am wrapped in glorious, golden wonderment and
        joyfully greet the season.

March 20, 2018

Poetic Justice

Resolution of a life

Writing poetry

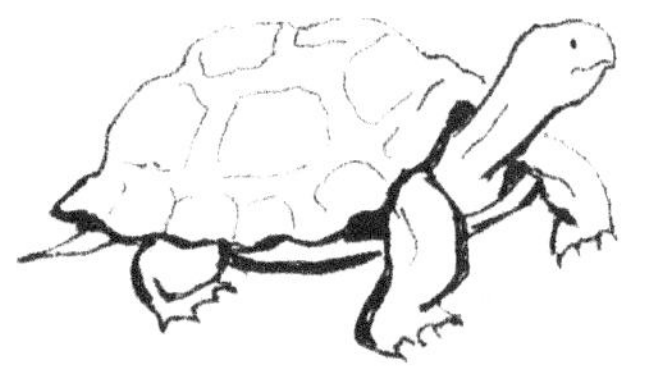

Marching Orders

Here now. There then. A mix of past and present,
        seasoned with just a dash of hopeful future glances.
Do not wait to do what impassions you
        so NOW creates no hollow PAST
                and FUTURE presents no incline.
Indeed, give in to inclination. Charge on with noble soul.
Fulfill divine purpose.
We are near to give a hand
        to raise you up and stand in ovation.
This promise enacted fills all Pasts.
Each in turn, we become the "us" in tremendous,
        and grow mighty.

March 7, 2014

Nurturance

Open the doors of your temple, the pores of your skin.
Absorb the wonder, breathe it in, gulp it down.
Witness its radiance, hear its blessed symphony.
Fill up, fill up, fill up to overflowing,
        to have, to give to those you meet along the street.
Its presence palpable, it calms, excites, rewards, delights.
Circle, spiral, vortex of might.
Ever-giving, as we are living, constant, true,
        here for me, for you, unending Soul Food.

February 16, 2014

Where have you Been?

In this book lie words of erstwhile visits from poems,
    full-blown, demanding to be immortalized
        with my pencil on this paper.
A mind, jumbled by daily ploddings and demands,
    writes only lists of things "to do" on bits of paper scrap.
When will soul words arise from the ashes of chore words,
    long ago burned up by mundane motions,
        to receive new poetic intrigue, new babblings
           from bountiful brooks, new sparks of joy,
             grief, wonderment, anger, reverie?
I await, with eyes and mind and spirit open,
    pencil poised in urgent anticipation.
I know those words are waiting in patient lines, angling for
    arrival, position and purpose to fulfill their destinies
    upon the page.

March 7, 2018

And So It Goes

Art turns Art.
Commerce turns Commerce.
Community turns Community.
Humanity turns Humanity.
And so it goes.
We change from the inside.

March 15, 2018

A Spire

A Spire
Aspire to reach that dangerous place, that sharp peak of
      wealth, of fame, of spirit.
Altitude...the heights where few fit with ease, with grace,
      with gratitude.
Attitude...descends too swiftly to hubris, to smug boasts,
      to entitlement.
No eye of needle permits passage of such obesity.
Oh, to flow through with glorious liquidity, as silken thread
      might twine itself beyond, with all that baggage.

November 4, 2018

Above the Clouds

Ah, to see from the sunshine side of the clouds!
Rise above the angst of dark self, see beyond the next page.
May I continuingly soar through clear skies of faith,
      of surety, as my yearning to touch divinity buoys my
      body through this tangible plane.
This image of being fall-safe, with bubbling, bright-white
      cushions to break imagined graceless tumblings . . .
This image is what keeps me aloft.
I act the part, fervently, in hopes that I and it will melt and
      meld and weld together in permanent true bondage.
The mire and maelstroms of this life threaten my journey
      at every corner.
It is no simple task to remain true, but a worthy one.
I endeavor to keep this focus, to remain in flight
      on the sunshine side.
May I be, perhaps, a guide?

But it is not for me to make such promises,
        take such risks of ego blindness.
It is my journey, for me to take, in truth, alone
        but with Grand Accompaniment.
The music of the spheres resounds in my ears.

January 16, 2019

As Life Moves on

Loved One to Love Done.
Watch how footprints, once close, parallel, begin divergence
        by millimeters, then miles,
            til distance, too great,
                breaks the connector thread.
Ties broken, paths move in opposition, at odds, rancorous,
        hearts torn and aching.
This earthquake of emotion leaves chasms too great to cross,
        cross back, cross over.
They will remain as deep reminders of love too shallow
        to sustain the strain of heavy passages.
BUT, gentle, joyous journeys await ahead.
It is as life moves on.

Manuka

I snoozed the alarm this morning, but grief denied
        return to restorative sleep.
The blanket of sorrow weighs heavy on me now.
I long for the weight of soft cat feet for my ritual awakening,
        the get-going paw pushing at covers, unmoving, now.

The plaintive Siamese yowl is stilled, as well.
So quickly the downward spiral took him to the point where
        very little life was left, when "the decision" made itself.

Mourning in the morning strikes as an alarm bell and rouses
        the dreamless sleeper.
We bury Manuka today, beside Pharaoh and Shanti, a sacred
        space for those loved and lost.
Ah, those four-leggers!
How they seep into cells and souls of those two-leggers
        who "own" them.
We know that four is greater than two. They always own us.
Not now, but in time, there will be others to love.
Rest assured.

February 3, 2019

Emergence

Feeling fragile, I watch another piece of me fracture and
        fall to the floor.
I watch, in ambiguous fascination, the clutter of chips and
        chunks littering the space around me.
A glacier, destined to calve its bergs into the sea of
        separation, splashes upon mind vistas.
I am no glacier, just a little woman, sorrowful, repentant.
Truly, this shedding smacks of shells broken to release the
        promise of fresh, feathered existence.
I yearn for this emergence, naked, new, fearless, spotless,
        an infancy of me, authentic, pure, unencumbered,
                peaceful, acquiescent.
Perhaps . . .tomorrow . . .I'll fly

April 20, 2012

When I was a Pipsqueak

When I was a Pipsqueak
With an ego that couldn't possibly fit inside my body, but
      wrapped around me in spider webs of selfie-ness,
          my "knowledge," was worn like a weapon to
            wield indifferently on the unsuspecting.
Not wanting to hurt, or humiliate, or trump, not knowing
      how sharp its blade could be, wield it I did.
"Ah callus youth," they might say.
"Ah careless fool," I now say, retrospect finding its target.
Now, with more life under my belt, my stomach tightens
      with shame at that spouting arrogance.
But let me build compassion for myself.
Withhold judgement on the youth of today.
They, too, may feel the sting of retrospect, in due course.
May the grace of wisdom mete out forgiveness.
           June 8 & 27, July 6, August 4, 2019*

*See how life will take its time before we come to that place.

I Tend to Grief

I tend to grief.
It barges in upon the scene as does death, so often.
It knocks me down mid-stride with a depressive cloak that
        suffocates gladness.
Though I seem to accept its presence, its malaise,
        debilitating and cumbersome,
                it compels me to cast it off with urgent prayer.
In darkness, a deep well of joy enlightens gratitude
        for what is always mine,
                like multi-colored helium balloons,
                        that carry a sorry soul beyond the mire.
So it seems there is a rise in the fall.
                                August 2022

We on bended knees

Deep humble human vision

Scan the gloom for stars

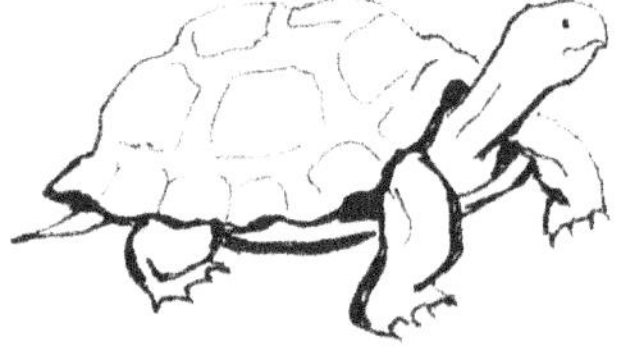

Bumpy Roads

And so, it goes...the journey plagued by bumpy roads,
    the path a juggernaut, challenging every move,
        routes misdirected.
G.P.S. - unreliable techno help, out of order.
Oh, that it were a God Protective System!
Getting lost too easy, spatial senses skewed, physical,
    emotional, spiritual collisions almost inevitable.
Is it me?
Is it the world of this moment, so out of balance,
    so asynchronous?
Head wanting.   Heart yearning.
Misunderstandings. Bumps, Bangs, Bruises.
Oh, for a magic wand to smooth the path.
Oh, for the Great Arms to hold us close,
    to feel their strength and comfort!
Body, Heart, Spirit, distance felt so keenly, even close ones
    cannot salve the wounds.
Self-inflicted? Accidental? Deliberate?
Is this a common affliction?
Is this all a Cosmic Churn tumbling us hot and dry
    in an act of communal cleansing?
If it be so, let us hold each other in tight embrace,
    in desperate comfort of spirit melding,
        of soul healing love.

September 12, 2019

Sham

Who is this sham of a person?
Who walks in this body, speaks with these lips?
Pretending . . .
Presumptuous . . .
Preposterous!
Is there even one genuine atom to be found?
I suspect not, though some are fooled into believing.
Sham.   Shame.
A good actor, but a fake, even at that.
How dare she do that?
A blip on the big screen, a guise, a masquerade.
Pay no attention to that person behind the curtain.
It is merely a figment of imagination, less real than that
        speck of blood from the mosquito you just slapped.
Wipe your hand and go on your way.
The blackest of thoughts fill her mind.
She cannot let you know her reality.
Whatever it seems to be will crumble before your eyes.
Pathetic picture of writhing self-loathing,
        even as she wrestles with authenticity.
Currents of disappointment surge within.
A puny, sorrowful soul awakens each day to trudge through
        her own sludge in hopes of hope.
Ah, but I'm being self-indulgent.

September 27, 2019

Times

Now there's no time to let the mind wander,
    exploring thoughts beyond the grind.
No time to climb mountains of imagination,
    nor dive the subterranean caves of Guilt and Grief.
To write the newnesses of experience is for women of leisure,
    those possessed by the feel of pencil strokes on paper.
Not for me, not now.
The Cosmic churn that swirls around the planet
    has not missed this house.
We ride waves of change on old surfboards,
    and could face-plant into gritty sand.
Yet, old and challenged by the unfamiliar, we determine
    to maintain our footing, our balance, to meet
        the shifting of our tectonic plates each day.
We are not done yet with the toil of life.
And look! I'm writing this today.
The poet's soul may be shoved aside of necessity but
    give me a phrase in a waking moment, and my hand
        mounts this pencil to gallop across this page.

November 20, 2019

Love

As blood flows, so does love, through veins beyond ourselves,
    to nourish bodies and souls.
Fret not. Ask for more. Always given. Never withheld.
Abundance unending.
Love, the emblem of Life, foundation of Unity.

November 30, 2019

Come Together Now

Coalescence
Convergence
Merge-ence into
Cohesive unity of One.
Warm peace
Solace
Comfort
Tranquility
Sublime Fearlessness.
Ah! I have arrived.

August 2011

Erase the Slate Now

Erase the slate now.
Sweep away this pains-taking, pain-giving sand painting,
        drawn with such meticulous, detailed,
                grain-by-grain precision.
Blow down the card house built with such obliviousness to
        its obvious flaw, its foundation upon a fault-line
                poised to slip.
Leave behind left-over tension from the fabrication of fragile,
        fictional constructs.
Fall, Rag Doll, to the floor.
Accept culpability. Become compassion.
Cease hostility. Defy denial.
Fulfill forgiveness.
Grow into the empty spaces of your fabric.

They say life is too short.
Indeed, it is when clinging to mis-takes.
Shake them off.
Erase the slate now.
Build anew with me, sister.

September 2011

A Renga

I am a cloud of dust
Swirling on the winds of life
I spread myself thin

Barely cohesive
Dusting ev'ryone I meet
I mark my essence

Your dust is my dust
We mingle as we commune
Weaving soft blankets

We think we've settled
Breezes set us off again
More mixing to do.

There are no mistakes

Just detours to becoming

Becoming ourselves

Peace Space

Sun's rays upon my face, liquid light floods my being.
Bright golden circles just behind closed lids
        turn to deep indigo and melt away tight molecules.
Deep respiration empowers, dumping inner toxic waste
        landing at my feet, heavy, sodden, dank.
Walk away.
Leave it there to decompose.
Now to recompose my atomic self, my cosmic self, shifting
        into new con-firm-ity.
Now, keep this flowing.
Know this feeling.
Return when life spins out of control again.
It is always there.
Once found, this firm foundation of spirit strength is a
        constant, present, gift, verity undeniable, delicious,
                heavenly sustenance.
Unbounded, unending, uncompromisable.
Trust. Step into this space of sunshine.
The door is open.
I'll take your hand . . . if you wish.

October 6, 2011

It's All Good

Last night it rained. Florida rain.
Surprising, hard, drenching rain.
We huddled together as if it would make a difference,
        but the lightning, the thunder, the wind pushed
                everybody into a ball of US.
Felt better, safer, drier, even, like that.
It's OK.
Today the sky is blue clear.
The sun is golden warm.
Dry fresh breeze, for now where we live.
We walk to the One Stop.
Food, a shower, hey, laundry!
Martha runs this place.
Tough little stick!
Always overalls and plaid cotton shirts, ready to work.
She's been here, where we are now, only deeper, darker.
She knows us like the back of her hand.
We don't get away with ANYTHING!
And it's all good.
We get IDentified, maybe snag a short gig somewhere,
        make a few bucks.
Some of us snag a bus ride home,--
Mississippi,
Massachusetts,
Pennsylvania--
Other states with longer names, longer and colder winters,
        but HOME if we want.
And it's all good.

Hey! maybe some TV dude'll do a show called
        "Lifestyles of the Poor and Unknown."

My buddy, what's-his-name, thought'a that one.
But most of us just want to be full not frantic, ya know?
Grateful, not greedy, satisfied not over-sated.
Blanche DuBois said,
        "I've always relied on the kindness of strangers."
I know my Tennessee Williams.
Other than my buddies, that's where kindness comes from.
Kind, good, generous, helpful people.
They don't know us; we don't know them.
A smile. A handshake. A recognition.
We're family.
And it's all good.

August 2011

Transformation

Picture profile platinum blond pouting little girl sitting sad at
        tableside.
Birthday party, not hers, not jealous, just inconsolable.
Ice cream melting into cake, uneaten.
Shrieks and giggles surround, not contagious,
        a kicking, cacophonous wall of isolation.
Unforgettable.
Future frames reflect this first empty-heartedness
        smacking of soul schism, separation.
Eroding deep canyons echoing watery sighs ending nowhere.
Now here. Now there.
Senseless, useless, worthless, time spent.
Self-indulgent, grief-wallowing habit.

Now breaking bonds, clambering wildly,
        to willfully fulfill little girl yearning dreams.

Side view silver blond stretching senior
        striding 'round bends, twists turns, ups downs,
            roller coaster ride of her Life!
Undaunted.
It's about Time!

July 2011

Transcendence

Trusting her breath to carry her, she passes through the
        room, not touching the floor.
She sees the self she was at ten, framed on the wall.
So many sitting in chairs set out for this occasion.
The wedding was just like this, percolating joy.
Now beyond tangibility, she observes them all
        battling brittle grief.
How she yearns to comfort.
"This is greater joy," she whispers in their ears.
None but the child hears. A smile appears.
His breath softens. She departs.

Poetess Princess

Impede the impish impulse.
Propel the precious purpose.
Inspire insightful intellect.
Oh, those words!
How they fit so finely, snap together so simply, so smartly,
    so seamlessly.
Poetic promises precisely placed, professional, perhaps.
They thrill my thoughts, fidget with philosophy,
    fly about faith, carry me to conclusion:
This poet's printing passion, prickling with pride,
    proves a perfect point -
Sharp,
Sassy,
Show off.

October 30, 2011

Ode, to be a Butterfly

Oh caterpillar!
I much prefer the life of a butterfly.
You, clambering in determination to destiny, voracious,
    insatiable appetite.
Greedy for greenery, razor jaws munching, crunching leaves
      into serrated oblivion until, bursting and ready to
         explode, that last morsel consumed,
           action shifts to chrysalism,
Brilliant self-mummification.
Now still and silent, sated and set for certain transformation.
Metamorphosis from clumsy climber to fluttery flier,
      wings and winds lifting aloft dandelion yellow,
         indigo blue or Hari Krishna orange Delight.
I, the earthbound, stand spellbound in wonder, wanting,
      wishing, willing myself such surety of glorious change.
And then I know the Metamorphic Metaphor.
The caterpillar neither knows nor makes
      the molecular modification, as it devours the
         lusciousness of leaves.
It doesn't dream of life in flight.
It is, of course, only a lowly crawling grub.
And, once it is Butterflying, there is no thought of
      Caterpillaring.
And so, too, will be this life for me.

June 1, 2012

Betty

She's lying S-shaped, shrunken vision of herself,
        poised for departure.
Breathing and heartbeat belie death's proximity,
        her choice to let go.
One sigh closer now, the longed-for release is nigh.
We wait patiently. We will all be well.
We celebrate your living. We'll meet you later.

To the Last Breath

Right up to this much-anticipated brink, a step into Oblivion,
        it has been written:

   "When God leads you to the edge of the cliff, trust Him fully and let
go. Only one of two things will happen, either He'll catch you when you
fall, or He'll teach you how to fly."

Mmmmmm, Adventure? Soft landing?
Where do I sit at the Deserving Table?
Did I earn my just desserts? Was I good enough?
Kind enough? Generous enough?
Did I try hard enough? Were my thoughts pure enough?
Did I help? Did I hurt? Did I use my breath wisely,
        soothingly, compassionately, lovingly . . . enough?
Now this breath, shallow and short, promises to escape my
        lips one last time. No choice is given.
Just give in. To what, I know not, but here goes...
A.h.h.h.h.h...h...h...h........... . . . . .October 31, 2011

The past will not return

It shapes us with its twisting

We still can walk straight

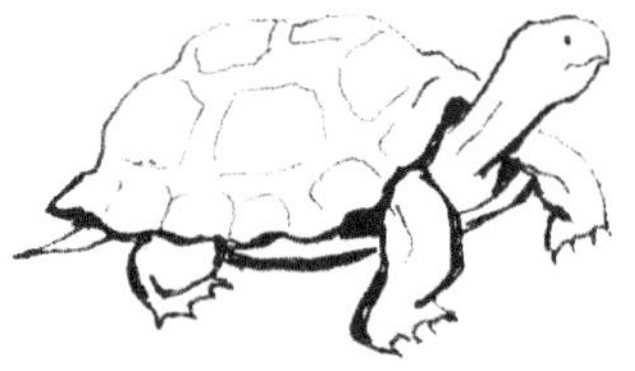

The All-timers

Memories drip from her like blood on to the carpet.
Slowly her life loses itself while she looks the other way,
      pursuing the tail of a recollection recently escaped
            from the mouse hole that is her mind.
Childhood escapades slip from her lips
      when I ask what she ate for lunch.
That familiar laugh, once so frequent,
      briefly brightens her pale brown eyes.
Beloved belongings, once known and cherished,
      now reduced to but a few in this small, drab space,
            have faded to insignificance.
I am sitting here, her hands in mine,
      searching the contours of her face for the crumbs of
            my own memories.
In the creases around her eyes, her mouth, I find
      only remnants of the morning's muffin.
She looks at me, with the slight smile that always graces
      her face.
It reminds me that I have pledged to reflect that
      loving countenance.
When she says, "Who are you?" my breath skips a beat
      and I tell her again,
            "I'm Laurie, your daughter, Mom. I love you."
The smile once more,
      a flash of questioning recognition, "I love you, too."
We look deep into the places where souls stir and
      nothing is lost, embrace the endless moment,
            breathe, in unison, knowing.

November 18, 2011

Arrow: A composition of multiple meanings

Arrow, launched from the bow of Heart and Soul.
Up she rose, composed herself a piece to play along the
      stream of Life and Love, to contemplate the passing of
      passings along the Spirit Path.
The arcing, aching journey's pointful accuracy
      strikes its target, breaking hearts open to
      receive its blessing.
Its message, its lesson . . ."I'm not afraid to die," and
      "the only way out is through."
We learn. . . the only way out is through,
      so we can be unafraid to die.

September 23, 2015

Thanksgiving Day: Nov. 22 ,2012

I sit in solitude, mindful of my fragile tangibility,
      willing myself to decompose, to disclose the essence of
      my being, that spirit that resides within,
      without material me.
The Me, the dust of earth, molded with Loving Hands,
      held in form with godglue, destined to dissolve,
      merely a place of temporary residence.
May I reveal, in sweet purity, my truth to you?
May I be the beacon that shines on you?
May I be the x-ray beam that clears your dust to
      discover our naked kinship, our spirit emergence,
      as bodies become redundant?

May you share my vision.
See the shapes of others slip to the earth.
Know their pure essence reflects our own.
Smash the complexity of "difference", and walk through
        its shards, barefoot, unscathed.
Arrive alive among the Family.
Manifest Peace.

And It Could Be So Easy

They turned the words to swords.
Now turn the swords into plowshares and tanks to tractors to
        roil the soil, to plant the seeds of unity, to reap peace.
Let head and heart and hands touch with beneficent
        brotherhood . . . serene sisterhood.
This could be so easy.
Lift the veils of concealment.
Reveal the warm, bright space that allows the "other" face
        to look like you . . . like me.
Seek harm to no one.
Let your steps lead to those in need, to lift them up,
        to fill their cups with not just soup, but grace.
And this could be so easy.
Gather joy from the immediate air and fill your cup so full
        that all you need to do is breathe and all around
            will spring into gladness.
And this could be so easy.
                    March 20, April 7, 11,17, 23, 2014

(Perhaps this is how it will move forward – baby steps.)

State of the Union

This image, unintentioned, unmistakable.
Red-striped symbol of nationhood shredded
    on nearby bushes.
Soaring eagle wired into jerry-rigged flag pole,
    now fallen from its perch.
It seems wearied from buffeting fights with elemental might.
Yes, yes, I hear the proud patriot's hyperbolic protests
    at this striking metaphor.
"America, the greatest!"
Ah, so was Rome.
The blindered eyes.
The hardened hearts.
Hubris, the classic symptom, turned ears deaf to the
    sighs of death.
And so it has again.
And so it has again.
This image, unintentioned, speaks volumes of truth.

April 30, 2012

(This is an accurate description of a flag on the property of a house
down the street from our home in Florida. I took a picture, but
somehow lost it, otherwise I would print it here.)

With This Breath

With this breath I pass my days.
With this breath I fill my lungs with oxygen to feed my blood,
        to nourish heart, mind and self.
With this breath I blow my kisses, filled with love that
        never misses its mark.
With this breath my prayers embark.
With this breath I share my life with you, and every you who
        enters my space.
A life of inclusion, no seclusion is mine as I live and breathe.

June 14, 2014

Belief

Belief is the relief that fills your cells
        and tells your soul to sing.

Courage

Courage is resolve to action.
Sit with self, learn the strength to make the moves
        undaunted.

August 15, 2014

Vultures

This old house on the creek - its boarded windows
      tell the tale.
In this holiday season, though,
      its roof peak is lined with a string of flights
        illuminating the fatality of an
          erstwhile residence, now dead.
Those dark, glowering turkey vultures would, if they could,
      devour it, peck by bloody peck.
This old house, upside down, under water, undeniably
      stamped with that eleven-letter "F" word.
These birds thrive on its rotting wetness.
Some wings stretch out to catch sun and wind to dry.
Others, drawn tight against sides, wingtips in pockets,
      heads retracted like turtles, looking to all the world like
        dark-suited, greedy bankers.
En masse, in sudden dismount, the hook-beaks circle-swirl
      in search of better pickings.
I think I hear the ravished rooms cry out in anguish.

Today, dark shadows crisscross the stretch of sand and
      weeds we call our back forty.
They are here now, over our home, this old house,
      Florida cracker.
One hundred and one years have flown since hot Florida
      drafts flowed round its fresh wooden studs.
Now, in disrepair, updrafts of sorrow gush from doors and
      windows to draw these great birds to it.
Their proximity stigmatizes.
What they do is not their fault.

They are drawn to death.
It is their purpose.
But we live here still.
We keep this old house alive with our presence.
We hold it dear, we cherish it, with our hands, our voices
        our sweat, our breath.
I shout, "Go away, go away and don't come back!
Goawaygoawaygoawaygoaway!"
My voice grows hoarse. They hear.
They sense they cannot perch on our roof peak --
        not today.
They circle-swirl and head
        north?
        east?
        west?
        south?
Hungry eyes know the wealth of these perching places
        in this time.
They'll be back . . .
Just checking . . .
I'll shout them away again, and again and again and again,
        until I am no longer here.

December 18, 2011

Thoughts on this "'Tis the Season"
(a poetic non-poem holiday greeting)

Look back a bit at this Thanksgiving.
Did misgivings evaporate?
Did missteps redirect to harmonic roads for reconciliation,
    to spirit openings upon trails where trials are
        left behind?
Our wish, that this is true to some degree, at least,
    flies on hopeful wings to friends, to family, to all.
May this "'Tis the Season" celebrate with cheerful charity,
    joyous generosity and gladsome gifts, no tags attached.
Greetings from hearts to spirits wrapped in comfort, in love.
Peace in your hearts.

                        December 20, 2013

For the Love of For

That word "for"
How can three soft letters carry so much weight?
I wait for hours.
I yearn for love.
I stand for independence.
I cry for peace.
And then, like the remora, it attaches,
    apparently permanently, to the shark words,
        bear and swear, give and get, go and stall,
            bid and fend.

That mutating hue-altering chameleon of a word, almost
        unnoticed, sly and conspiratorial, to alter meaning,
        character, though its characters remain
        unchanged.
How does it dare to be so small and insignificant,
        to hold such power?
Do I dare to draw comparison?
Can I-you-we transform, transmute, translate from our puny
        forms into more than we suspect, to subtly sabotage
        character, intention, meaning?
More than Magic . . . yes . . .
Manifestation of Might.

Kid Time

When I was a child, the past was put precisely
        BACK THERE.
When I was a child, the future fit firmly ahead
        FAR AWAY.
Yesterday I found now is as close to was as to be,
        the to be of was and the was of to be.
Looking linearly, we forever move from past to future
        through **TIME.**
But looking **ALL AT ONCE**, all bets are off.
The Power of Now.

                                    Undated....curious....

How to....

Judging and grudging
 Building barriers
  Closing doors
   Cutting off noses
    Shooting our own feet.
That's how it's done, folks,
Unwitting recipe for bitter loneliness.

      June 10, 2016

Thoughts

Life is a series of interruptions along the earthly path that
 give us opportunities to reflect and redirect the course
  we've plotted.
Sometimes, the gifts found in hindrances lead us to
 True North.

      November 26, 2020

Hard as steel foulmouthed

Felon-Rapist-Murderer

Born a Child of God

Standing at the Edge of Myself

Go right in.

Huh?

It's OK, nothing to fear, my dear.

But I . . .

Go on, go on.

Mmmmmmmmmm . . . O. K.

Deep breath, step one . . . OH!
Squishy, dark, purple, . . . grape? . . .Jell-O?!?!
Step two . . . EWW!
Lumps!   ooh,   oops!   slippery.
It jiggles and sucks itself around my legs.
Hard going, this!
These lumps!
UGH! I know.....the obligatory fruit salad.
Cubed pears, peaches, halved grapes . .bananas?
         ....cherries?
What does all of this mean?
Green grapes of guilt?
Gritty pear fears?
Clingy peach grief?
Diced disillusionment?
WAIT, wait, wait, wait . . . now I'm scared.
Run! Run! Don't look back!
Yikes! STUCK!!!!
BUT . . . WHY?

No danger here.
No sharp teeth.
No catching claws.

No weapons.
AND . . .
I'm a grown-up!!
What is this anyway?
Nothing but a Jell-O mold, an old and moldy Jell-O mold.
I will conquer it, this wordless mass, this wriggling,
        sucking muck!
JELL-O WRESTLING!?!?
Arrrrrrgh, it is elusive,
Slipping from my grip, making me slide.
OW!!! . . . this isn't working!
AHA! I break the fourth wall.
I look at you all, and say, in whispers, so "it" doesn't hear,
"I'll get my spoon."
Ingestion – the ultimate weapon in this battle.
So easy, death by MASTICATION. I begin.
Chewing, chewing   swallow.
Chewing, chewing   swallow.
My, but there's a lot of stuff here!
UGH! yet again.
I am gagging on this.
Overwhelming smell, so cloying.
This meal, this battle, this eating bout is not for just
        one sitting.   Sigh!
I'll be back, you beast!
I will integrate you into me.
I will know you.
I will own you. I will have slain the Jell-O-wockey, my son.
(Ridiculous poem, I know, couldn't help myself. . . .

All in Good Humor. . . . now that sounds delicious.)
Now, I will be full of myself.
Now, I will have pulled myself together.
Now, I will be a force unto myself.

And you, dear reader, go right in.
It's OK, nothing to fear, my dear.

August 3-13, 2013

Playfully Yours

Don't ask me why
I am high.
Though I am shy
I like to fly.
I will sigh
When I buy
This for my guy.
Please don't pry!
It's on the sly
So he will cry
Oh my, my, my,
I love this tie!
My humor's wry.
I often try
To make him die
Laughing.
I won't deny
When he draws nigh
I hit the sky.
You mustn't vie
To catch his eye
Or I might ply
My deadly chai
Or lethal stye
Or make you fry
In bubbly lye,
Eat poison pie.
I'm really spry.
I don't know why.

December 27, 2011

Life Renga

Driftwood drift would I
I would if I could drift on
No destination

Thinking of nothing
Reaching for no illusion
Marking journey's days

A feather on wind
A leaf on rippling stream
A kiss on my breath

If I pass near you
I will slip through your fingers
Leave no impression

It is meaningless
This talk of disconnection
It's impossible

This world of roses
Thorns do snag and drag us in
They imprison us

Til we grow strong wings
Til we have sturdier legs
We await release

The tangle of lives
Fabric of humanity
Enfolding us here

Spell out our purpose
The design of our mission
We live 'til we die

A Remembrance of Wind

It is a soft, warm wafting across the face,
    sun still winterish.
It is hope.

It is a chilly gust, an autumn warning,
    as sun begins its southward arc.
It is change.

It is the hot smack
    on a bristling summer day.
It is passion.

It is the screaming blizzard howl
    forcing souls to bend against it.
It is challenge.

When it is still,
    its blessings hidden,
It is peace.

January 21, 2020

Waiting in Patience Like the Cat
at the Beginning of its Nine Lives

Now writing when life is full of emptiness, the hollow
        in my chest swallows me into its darkness.
I grow still. The vacuum sucks the energy from my limbs.
Thoughts dissolve to
        word
                -less
                        -ness.
A dull and silent state of being. . . .
        the weight is great upon my chest, my gut.
This grave of grief I call my life, this sad charade that
        I am fine, this manic masquerade in which I dress
                myself and stumble through my days.
I am playwright, director, actor.
I write, stage, rehearse my role so well very few see through
        thick, now cracking, greasepaint and ancient powder.
I am good at this. . . . .

When did I begin?
Time before memory? Was I born to mourn,
        meant to live loss from my mother's womb?
This grief I carry clouds my days, mutes my joys, mocks my
        laughter with its own gloating grin.
It knows its own vaporousness.
This mourning, it is conundrum, it is enigma.
I suspect it is the ache of my own emergence from
        what I was before and longing to return,
BUT, I must wait. I can wait. I will wait, and
        play the role I know so well I almost believe it.
                                        February 6, 2012

Spring Cleaning

Let me purge this dark and dismal GRIEF, this sticky,
        depressive affliction.
Help me scour the walls and corners of my psyche.
Help me hunt it down to the interstices in which it hides,
        eradicate its presence, even to its last atom.
I know, if I am not vigilant, its regeneration will
        overwhelm me again, again and again.
BUT, I will climb this mountain of dank debris to breathe the
        crisp breezes of release, to scan the horizon of grace,
                to feel the freedom of unfettered joy,
                        to know grief-less-ness.
THEN, back to broom and brush and disinfectant
        to purge its cousin, GUILT.

Who Shall Remain Nameless

Silent little soul, when did you arrive?
It was a moment I wasn't tuned to hear my soul strings
        strummed as you passed by to take up residence
                within me, a moment, off guard.
I never felt the force of life surge from toes to head.
But there you were, quiet, fragile, simple, your elementary
        complexity having eased into my essence like a thief
                of my body, my mind, my heart, my soul,
                        a short-term parasite.
What I ate, what I drank, what I did, what I didn't do,
        was all with you in mind.
Possessed I was, certainly.

Meditation, in retrospect, summoned from my
        inner chambers only echoes of my own thoughts.
Questions asked of you returned unanswered,
        so quiet were you.
Seven weeks . . . when was it?

Another moment when I wasn't listening, you stole away
        as silently as you came.
Ten weeks, the moment indelible, unmissed, the matter
        which was you passed from me.
"Products of conception" I was told.
Tonight, in darkness, I lie nursing your sister.
My body screams out its grief, bursting from my open mouth
        silently, like your brief journey.
Silently, because the deepest pain has no voice.
Silently, so your father will sleep.
He will meet his grief in his own time, his own way,
        with and without me.
I can't, I won't, pour my pain on him, not now.
The names we pondered fall into ether, unclaimed.
Your absence we feel more keenly than your presence.
How odd it seems, yet not so odd.
"Peace. Be with God."
The only motherly advice I'll ever give you.

July 29, 1987

Soundscape

Being here, I hear the bamboo-bending breeze, clicking,
        squealing soundscape, the waterfall rushing,
                fountain flowing, Osprey soaring, loudly calling
                in silent skies.
Train's distant warnings join with dreaming dogs
        sleep barking, feet chasing phantom rabbits.
Breath on mute, senses on high alert, I hear my own
        heartbeat, my inner words as I compose myself.
                                October 26, 2012

What's Going on Here, 2020?

Earth is spinning on its axis and its ass, all the time,
        pondering the conundrum--which way is up?
Big decisions take time, and were it not for those outlandish,
        outrageous, out-of-their-minds humans,
                jumping about like fleas irritating her skin,
                        this wise, old natural wonder would have
                        figured it out in no time flat.
                                December 1, 2020

Tranquil waters flow

Refresh my deepest presence

Cleanse atomic bits

**Zimmerman Family Poem:
Written during a hurricane**

Laurie   Fred   Zoe   Jamie

Zoe: Mother Hurricane whines with gusts of must
          need settle down love bites.
          Alone - asleep in a world inside chaos alive.
Jamie: Until we become one with the chaos and thrive
          inside for an eternity of time with no escape.
Fred: I long for a moment of clarity to take me away
          from this mish-mash of repetitious thoughts and
          actions.
Laurie: The swish, the swash, of wind and rain beats out
          the rhythm of life's domain.
Zoe: We only seem to remain the same.
          Change screams with each wind rhyme, with each
          drop of rain, the trees chime.
Jamie: They cry out in, not pain, but Freedom.
          Each blast of wind they shudder joy, and I want some.
Fred: Some what? Some more excitement?
          More air? More time? Oh, settle down, and make the
          most of this moment.
Laurie: The best of this moment, the rest of this moment,
          becomes the test of a moment when it is well spent.

*I couldn't resist entering this exercise in family writing. It
was great fun for us during one of the hurricanes that blew
through Florida during 2004 or 2005.

Digging Deep

We live our lives on rocks and roots.
The earth itself speaks its history of ages gone by,
    long before us.
Appalachian land, worn rounded by rain and wind,
    heat and cold, sings the ancient melodies.
I am reminded by its dense constancy of how new I am at
    seventy-five, digging to plant fresh growth -
      a gingko - the ageless tree - this tree of Memory,
        dedicated to Mom, -in Mother Earth.
Gingko Biloba, that lyric name, nestles now in its new home,
    an excavated cavity, thick with roots of long-gone
      greenery and broken, tumbled ledges and quartz.
The slow violence of earth existence is made manifest.
Trees felled by age and insects, storms and lightning strikes,
    floods and fires, drought and disease, leave their
      nutrient veins clinging to the firm land.
Giant rock ledges, split by thermal battles, slowly become
    boulders, rocks, stones, gravel, sand.
I am delighted by their shapes and colors, textures and heft,
    as they keep me grounded to an ephemeral connection
    with this living being – EARTH.
I, the stone carrier, leave my tiny marks in this massive,
    aeonic history.
I am left in awe and wonderment, humbled and grateful for
    the generosity of this Creation.
I, the Druid, know of trees' communal network through soil
    and rocks, and yearn to hear the voices and translate
    the language, that higher vibration beneath the
    earth which could TELL US SO MUCH!

In Life Distracted, root tendrils wrap themselves around
        my spirit, a virtual embrace to hold me close in
            Divine Unity.
In response, I weave my soul purpose to connect
        with all other tapestries.
Break not the strands.
Sew in stitches of laughter, of joy and beauty,
        with grateful heart and hands.
I know my destiny.   I honor these bonds.
I tread my path on roots and rocks.

May 21, 2020

So Far

Heaven-white clouds pass below us.
Below them stretches the flat, geometric prairieland.
I know, as I gaze through pressurized window, my pupils are
        tight, black dots in my green irises - a painful struggle
            to adjust to almost unbearable lightness.
Thirty-five thousand feet above the land, it's as if I am
        looking at the Sun, so bright it is.
What can I learn from this in the Age of Corona as the world
        holds its collective breath, in fear or angry denial,
            as protests roil in the streets over
                age-old injustice, the never-ending
                    division and otherness of skin color?
What is held in this vista that pains my eyes with
        green of growth, red of soil, black of winding rivers?
Our westward direction takes us over rising hills and
        jutting mountains. I am in awe of its magnificence.
The country I call home, the land that stands bold and true,

tells of the scouring of glaciers, oceans now drained,
evaporation of centuries.
And I see God in every detail, every thought that
comes to consciousness.
From this journey I learn of my invisibility, my significant
insignificance, a mere strand in the Grand Tapestry,
woven together, ever connected, ever-changing,
evolutionary.
No distance.   No time.
Earth   sky   filled with astonishing beauty.
Pain, grief, anger, hatred, distrust, antagonism,
all threaten to tear apart the glorious creation.
We do not know our place!
Is it not to be in harmonic resonance with ALL?
Can it not be obvious that we are better than this?
Can we not drop our weapons and words to embrace
true fellowship - believe, trust, absorb the hidden
gifts of grace offered in the challenges?
They are there to bring it all together.

June 17, 2020

Let the River

Remove the boulder too long wedged.
Release the estuary too long stagnant.
Let it flow into the ever-cleansing river.
Our journey must be free and fresh, unfettered.
Light thoughts keep us afloat in shallow, rocky stretches.
Fearless focus keeps us steady in roiling rapids.
Know well that portage is possible. . .

There is no shame in camping on the shore to rest, refresh,
    renew, and reconstruct our vessel, to resurrect our
        flagging faith, to gain new perspective from
            dry and solid ground and return to our
            common journey.
Let the River carry burdens too great to bear.
Let the River teach us how to flow, to fathom
    depths of peace in tranquil waters.
Let the River merge us into Oneness.
Let the River move us to departure at the
        Delta of Great Mergence and Release into the Sea.
                                    January 24, 25, 2014

This Country

This country puts itself on a pedestal so distant from itself
        it cannot hear its own weeping,
            will not smell the stink of its own corruption,
                prides itself before its own fall.
Sit down here, honey, we gotta talk.
                                    February 12, 2021

Wednesday Rain

And now we have the tears of heaven to help us mourn
        what was before.
The future has never seemed so challenging.
The past now acknowledged as never to return.

Compassionate hearts of faithful friends are tangible pillows
	on which to lay our heads.
Gifts of Grace and Mercy hold us up on either side
	as we stumble under weights of grief and mourning.
Breathe deep the flowered air, breaths of love and kindness.
Revive the spirit that knows no boundaries,
	uplifted on the breezes of certainty.
This time, this transformation, will mark,
	with nuanced notes, the fullness of promise.
Know the touch of God is on our shoulders.

April 29, 2020

The Gathering: A Meditation

Circle round the pool of Grace in this peaceful valley.
Eyes meet in long and open gazes, ears alert to sighs and
	songs, hearts set in harmonic rhythm.
Step, in unison, into its cool, pure wetness to offer ourselves
	to its familiar essence, to merge our seventy percent to
		its one hundred.
Inhale the fragrance of green freshness, and
	enter, more deeply.
Become buoyant in its calm embrace as it cools us to
	a common heat.
Allow
Acquiesce
Surrender.
Know this as Truth.

September 13, 2020

A Musing

On this weighty date, 9-11, two points rise on my horizon.
Tears spring to my eyes, heart-twisting, mind-bending notes
        strike soul chords as I recall this day's significance.
First, the stripping of life-long hesitance startles me awake.
The words, "I can ask for what I want,"
        blur my vision with their permission.
The allowance of requests unmade in fear of rejection,
        distrusting my worth.
Who says what I deserve?
I diminish myself in false humility and ask not.
Yet I know what is on my list – not money, but enough to live,
        not power, other than what I hold over self,
          not fame unless it raises all to equal station.
"I can ask for what I want."
How else will it be known to all who will hear me?
Now the second spire of awakening rises into my musings,
        smelling sweetly in its simplicity.
"Pretending is okay."
I, the actor, remarks, "Of course, it's okay or I'd be out of work,"
        but I digress.
Pretending" - - not humbug, not dissimulation - -
        but practice, with heart attached, to play the role of
          human being human, to fuse cell matter with
            the gist of truth, kindness, generosity,
              peace in all abundance.
"Practice makes perfect," they say.
How else do we perfect ourselves, our world?
Let's pretend we like each other.
Let's pretend I am you and you are me.
Let's pretend to be peaceful.....
We can play at this until it's real. . . .perhaps. . . .
We can ask for what we want, it's okay.
We can pretend, it's okay.
We can WILL ourselves to change direction.
We will IF we will,
Then two bright spires can reach toward heaven. 2014

Spirit Child

Draped in the Ermine and Emeralds of Eternal Spirit,
    she walks silently through the bazaar.
What her soul holds is invisible to all but others who,
    like herself, are in league with the Divine.
Unknown, but not unfelt, the essence of that Ethereal gravity
    draws attention, with visceral magnetism.
No greetings, no salutations made, but reverence,
    akin to kneeling, permeates the crowd.
No words spoken, no need to speak, the message is clear.
The Spirit Child passage, the Ascension without demise,
    suffices to bless the witnesses.

December 27, 2020

Whose Love....

Whose love is it anyway?
Tis mine, for me, for thee, for any thee!
For thee with skin of black or white or Texas Dirt rust.
I give it freely, gladly.
It is mine to give, in generosity of spirit, indiscriminately.
It is yours to accept or discard.
But, though that is your choice, do not judge or dismiss
    this love as it flows and floats
        and follows its determined path.
For this love that is mine also is thine, and rhymes so sweetly
    with divine.
It is all, perpetual, this ever-accessible LOVE.

July 16, 2018

Petal soft fingers

Touch my brow my nose
my lips

Together we are

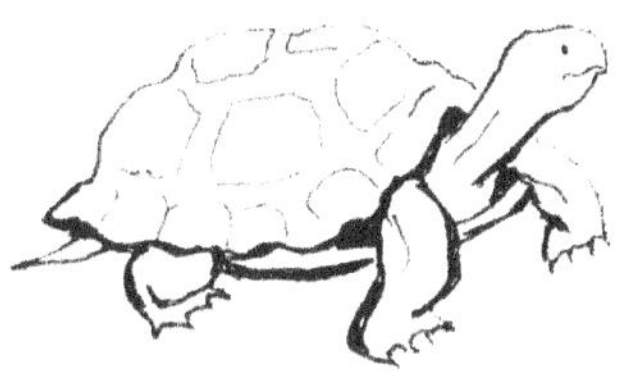

The Master's Passing: The Guardian's Grief

Soaked in sorrow, wrung out, yet hung to dry in the fresh
    breeze of Faith and the Golden Sun of Grace and Love,
Shoghi Effendi, walks the mountain passes finding solace in
    the magnificence of Blessed Creation.
In time, this drooping ensign of Service and Selflessness
    inhales sweet drafts of fortitude, of certitude,
        of strength.
He returns to that desk of Mountainous Responsibility
    to obey His Beloved, with dauntless dedication.
Ever burning bright in the fullness of devotion, it is the
    Sacred Submission.
Hours spent, no moment missed, fulfilling His purpose,
    the candle, undoused, til wax could provide no more
        fuel to the flame,
            spirit essence is all that remains.
Too soon they would say, but time, we learn,
    will have its way.
The Guardian's steps join the Grand Father
    in Joyous Reunion.

January 21, 2021

As Time Passes

My body tells me it is getting harder and harder to do the
    things asked of it in the past, those things it fulfilled
        nobly, with agility and strength and endurance.
I gloried in its performance like a strutting Derby racehorse.
I am bereaved by this loss of limberness, this lack of loyalty
    to my will.
I am bewildered that I am so irredeemably residing in this
    old woman's body.
I look at crepey skin that looks like that of crones with whom
    I never expected to catch up.
It was always a creepy thought to contemplate the age spots,
    the gross blotches from slight collisions with
        door jambs or cabinet drawers. Ugh!
My spirit tries to reconcile itself to the new old domicile,
    but it is foreign territory.
I do not know the language but know I will never master it.
So, I walk my walks, do my yoga and dance to Paul Simon
    and Bonnie Raitt, pretending my moves resemble
        those I turned when I was 27.
They don't, but I am joyful to feel the rhythm in my body,
    to shape my back to wrap itself around the chorus I
        sing out loud as I feel sweat slide down my spine.
The old girl ain't done yet, so don't talk to me about
    graceful aging and wisdom that comes with life lived.
My body will feel its way through times to come,
    find its balance through all the changes,
        and stride into the sunset as straight as
        my will can make it.
Don't you forget that, damn it.

April 28, 2021

In This Moment Renga

Breathe in this moment
Smell its vibrant fragrance
Scents of life's produce

Touch this moment's skin
Sense its sinew lies within
Pulsing power surge

Taste this moment's tang
Savor nuanced zestiness
Relish each instant

Be in this moment
No past no future just now
Fill it with your SELF

Eat this moment's meal
Turn succulence on your tongue
Soul food nutrients

Wear this moment's cloak
Wrap it warm around shoulders
Feel its protection

Sing this moment's song
Warble languid melodies
Pure-toned harmonies

Swim in this moment
Feel the surge of time and tides
Buoyant salt splendor

Kneading this moment
Shaping into what is true
Rising to meet you

Laugh with this moment
Human foibles at its heart
Cosmic joke fulfilled

Hearing this moment
Cacophony of voices
Symphonic straight talk

Chew on this moment
Contemplate its dense texture
Biting exercise

Take this moment now
A millisecond visit
Give it to yourself

In this moment's time
Its passage marks my journey
Endless space to roam

Sleeping Volcano

Found out. Ashamed. Chastised. Exposed. Defensive.
Efforts to fulfill the promise, to be the one who does it right,
who doesn't disappoint, who p.l.e.a.s.e.s,
lie tattered, with abrasions and bruises,
swollen with shame.
It doesn't take much.
The fissures, the fault lines, easily break through to
lava hot inadequacy bubbling beneath the
troubling masquerade – that lifelong charade
of having it all together.
Where is truth in this? Is there verity?
Is it all make-up, costumes and flimsy scenery?
All flagrant fabrication?
Not even she knows.

October 26, 2020

A Prayeroem

O God,
Help me to be humble in my path, loving in my demeanor,
generous in my service, joyful in my meetings,
kind in my touch, truthful in my response
and filled with trust and faith in
all my moments.
May I be a selfless servant in Thy World.

October 2020

26 Letters

3:30 in the mourning
Spelt the words
Sounded write
Know wonder
It maid no cents
Sew it seams
Maybe next thyme
When we meat again
It'll Phil the Bill
Kant sleep
Right it down
Fun Knee
Long knight

August 2022

Yes, this hast bean one of the weirdest peaces I halve ever writ ten.
P.S. Where honey is found?: Bee mine.

Matching

This is my breath, essential to life.
This my heartbeat—pulsing--moving matter to cells,
     the liquid essence of the Ocean of Being.
All this autonomous action without consciousness to guide,
     to even notice, its daily, grueling grind.
But as I give it mind, it appreciates its labors,
     enhances capacity, puts match to candles to light this
        Temple and radiate glowing life force.
In this present moment, I gift to you a whisper, a secret.
May I share this light, this warmth?
Will you strike your own illumination?
Muse upon this.　　　I am not the keeper of meaning.
March 5, 2014

It is there right now

Awaiting discovery

Anxious to meet you

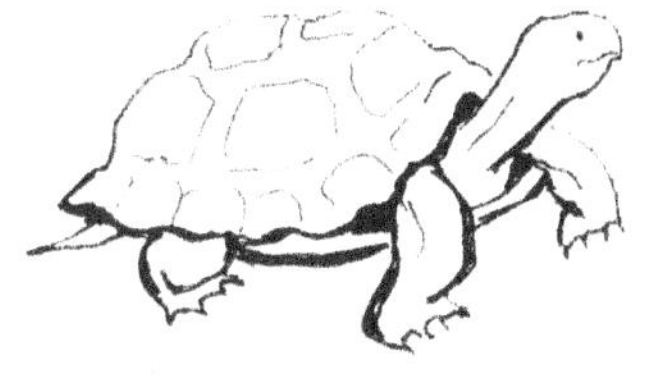

Indescribable

Life took me by the scruff of my neck, rushed
     my dangling self by scenes of hostility and hatred,
         torment and torture, strife and sorrow,
            where I would wallow given half a chance.
It dropped me on the deep salt sea of Itself.
There I could float as if I had no mass, like a feather,
     just simple spirit, buoyed by swells of sympathy and
         sacrifice, rapt in arms of comfort and
           compassion, taught to dwell in its
             warm, harmonic waves of joy
And to know its constant, accessible presence.

May 16, 2014

True Self

My body: my prison.
My mind: my jailor.
My emotion: my torturers.
My soul: my refuge, my resource, my reality.

June 12, 2012

My Self

This is my Self, scrambled sly Fem.
Not sly at all.
Woman, wondering, wandering, wading
     through world wilderness, wanting more,
        waiting even more, finding ways to become wise.

July 30, 2012

Clarine

White and tear-shaped, the petals fall around me in my yard,
 so many thousands of miles from where she passed.
From Arden, North Carolina to Adelaide, Australia,
 an agonizing aneurism away.
She is with us in flashes of unbelieving realization.
Her loss, of course, deeper now than when they left our hot,
 Florida neighborhood.
This is permanent.
This is irrevocable.
This is the end of imagining the two of them in that faraway,
 foreign land.
The new home meant for two, the long-awaited puppy
 meant for four-legger comfort and delight,
  the promises of deeper, firmer happiness.
He, oh friend, left bereft.
It breaks our hearts to realize the gaping emptiness in his.
"Why?" cries out from lips meant for kissing.
Faith and trust in God set aside, we want to shout,
 "You did this one wrong!
  This serves no greater purpose."
It all hurts so much, too far off for comfort to reach its arms
 around him.
Yet comfort we send on waves of prayer.
We are, we will be, with you, Bill.
Peace in your heart.

May 9, 2014

In Cool Green

I am.
I am.
I am a pond in the cool green glen, fed from below by clear,
     unending source waters.
I acquiesce to this gift as I overflow my banks with fingers of
     sweet freshness, that trickle to the valley below.
I am tranquil in this loss.
Filled with grace, becoming mercy, I pass my days in peace.
February 15, 2014

Thanksgiving 2020

On this day, filled with peace and grace,
     gratitude, heaped upon our plates, seasons the
          sweet air around this place, and gifts us with
               that deep sense of immersion into
                    Life and Family, large and small.
This gathering is made sacred by earnest thought,
     care and studied preparation.
It celebrates itself in meditative tasting of juices,
     tangible and intangible, floating in delicious hues, and
          wrapping themselves about our shoulders.
Such fine reasons for giving thanks.
November 26, 2020

Stuck

I stand, chin deep, in depressional muck, lift my face,
      raise my arms, sucking them out of the sludge of self
         to reach a finger hold on some thing beyond me.
My weakness now becomes my greatest strength.
Asking for help calls others to fulfill their purpose
      as they fulfill mine.
                November 26, 2020

For the Asking

I will not ask for love today, but for love to ask me to give it
      to all I pass along my way.
This irenic journey truly aimed toward peace,
      filled with potholes and pitfalls, challenges me.
But, when I think of diving into the deep, cool pools of love
      that never dry up, I carry hope in my satchel.
                November 11, 2020

Wishing

Wishing for you all sweet and refreshing sleep,
      a lullaby of prayer, gently calming all thoughts and
         turning them to God.
May heavenly fragrances fill your nostrils, and the most
      glorious music bless your ears.
Let there be a soft touch on your shoulders reminding you of
      how they will be made strong to carry your burdens.
Shine the Sun of deep faith upon you, always.
                Peace.

Beat my heart with joy

Give my spirit dancing room

Bless the air I breathe

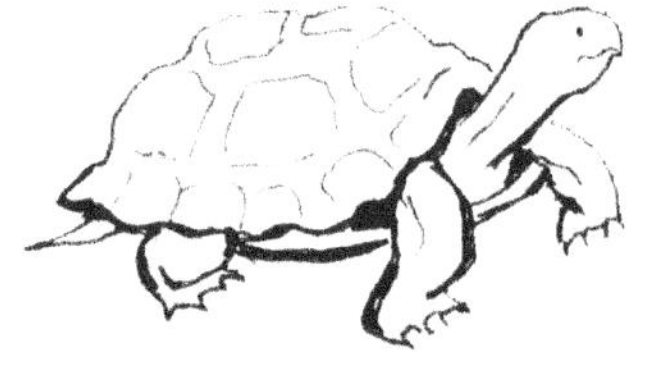

The Glorious Gang

On the borderline of balance, do not live on the edge of
     urgency, in the rush of reaction that tangles steps in
        wicked webs.
It propels the wayward into the darkness of insufficiency.
Now is the pandemic of the worst disease of fear, distrust,
     enmity, ignorance, the pandemonium that
        shakes the soil and tumbles truth.
As we cling to
     Honor – the banner,
        Faith – the shield,
           and Hope – the beacon,
              remember, the Center is in Us.
Weave the bonds that tether us together with enduring,
     compassionate cords.
We will form nothing less than a phalanx.
We will sing the hymns of celebration as one Glorious Gang,
     as one Undefeatable, as one Indefatigable Infantry.
In our Oneness is our strength.

                  October 17, 2020

Once Upon a Time . . .

Once upon a time, an ocean of time was poured out before
     me, a vastness as far as eyes can see beyond hearing,
       beyond mind reach.
Deep and pure.
Blue-green.
Untrammeled.
Pacific.
One blink and ripples radiate toward the horizon.
A hand raised stirs and generates whitecaps.
The slightest move stimulates this massive presence.
I am delighted and clap my hands in glee.
I giggle and jump with the joy of discovery.
I shout and dive in only to find myself sputtering,
     unable to navigate the swells.
I reach for help.
Is someone there?   Help!
Oh, it's you, the Time Maker.
Okay....okay, now.   so...will you teach me?
Will you be with me while I learn?
Agreed, I will try my hardest.
Already, behind me, remnants of time passed, rumpled and
     messy, a few neat packages, but... piles of time dust,
      unused or misused, along the edges.
Stunned at how much is wasted, I pledge to do better.
As I turn forward . . .WHAM! It hits me!
A giant wave filled with more than I could have foreseen.
Again, I am gob-smacked and reach out my hand.
It brings solid reassurance of ever-ready energy.
It pulls me up, sets me down, dusts me off, gives me hope.
I will do better.

In the beginning, the power felt when a blink could ripple the
        expanse,   OH, MY! It was ego expanding.
Now I expend great energy to stuff it down.
Time well spent. Humility the goal.

Can't resist checking up on progress, so I look back,
        hoping for less clutter in my wake.
Alas! It looks like times before.
There are more packages, even some with bows -
        some hastily tied with string or left open, but packages.
Lots of time dust.   I cough.
Can't sweep.....cough!
Can't do over, can't rearrange, can't delete –
        no button for that!
And I HAVE NO TIME FOR DUST!
Disappointment.
Each disappointment heaps upon the one before it.
It's all there in "The Record," the wastebasket filled with
        crumpled papers.
I kick it over and watch wads waft in little eddies on this
        landscape that clangs and rustles and drags behind me.
Inhale.   Exhale.   Patience the goal.
I reassemble my resemblance to an orderly,
        competent human being.
Hair and make-up. Check.
Clothing. Check.
Demeanor. Check.
Well done.
Onward!
I begin to see ahead of me Edges.
Hmmmmm
Odd . . .   or not so odd.
Had I been given "Forever?"

I couldn't have expected that much of a gift, or sentence.
After all, it was Thomas Hardy who wrote,

> "Measurement of life should be proportioned rather to the
> intensity of the experience than to its actual length."

Getting to the length part, I am, rolling along for a good
          many ticks and tocks.

Now I really must put my behind into it and
          "Try my hardest." Remember?
A promise is a promise.
So much to wrap up, complete, reconcile, tie up
          in packages,   with bows . . .

Overwhelm!
Resignation . . .
All of that may never be done.
And does any of it matter?
I have always had the Time Maker.
I haven't ever felt punished, except by myself.
I have loved and been loved, even in my imperfection,
          perhaps because of it.
I will do what I can -- the thises, the thats.
It is my promise.

Now, I will finish this poem, put it in a sweet little package,
          wrap it in pretty paper, put a big, beautiful bow on it,
                    and send it, with love, to you.
                                        January 17, 2022

******There were times in the past, that I, mostly, wrote songs. Many were for children, although there were love songs, as well. I include them here just because, while I'm at it, I might as well. The music is still in my head but, until books can be imprinted with sound, you'll have to make up your own tunes.

Come Along and Play

Come along and play, it's a holiday
Jumping rope, hop-scotch and swings
All 'n' everythings.
We can play our games today,
Eat an ice cream cone and back to
Swings and things, playing queens and kings,
Flying down a slippery slide,
Singing songs and playing
Hide and seek, tag, blind man's bluff,
Pick a posy, skip along,
There's a dandelion, go and
Puff it high, high into the sky,
Close your eyes so tightly now
For a wish to make.
We'll be like ice cream and cake.
You're a friend no one can ever take.

June 1966

Lullaby

Close your eyes,
Hush your cries,
Go to sleep my little one.
Close your eyes,
Hush your cries,
Sleep so soundly, little one.
Tender and mild
You are my little child,
I am so beguiled by your smile.
But now, close your eyes,
Hush your cries,
Go to sleep my little one.
Nursing warm
In my arms
Pleases and nourishes you.
Soon sugarplum fairies will come
To dance on the toe of your shoe.
Tender and mild
You are my little child,
I am so beguiled by your smile.
But now, close your eyes,
Hush your cries,
Go to sleep my little one.

For Ariel, 1973

A WALKING SONG

This is a walking song
A giggley walking song.
You sing it as you walk along
'Cause this is a walking song. GO!

Diddley-squat 'n' piggleywiggley, tiddle-de-wink, achoo!
Ridiculous words and phrases that
        keep you from feeling blue.
There's flibberty-gibbbet and alakazam, mares-eat-oats and
        thank you ma'am, razzmatazz and all that jazz
            and bibbity-bobbity   BOO!

There's ishkabibble and dibble-de dribble and snicklefritz
        and bug-in-a-rug, bump on a log and jiggedy-jog,
            gimme a hippomapatomus hug - mapotomus hug
                mapotomus hu-u-u-u-g ....

AGAIN!
Diddley-squat 'n' piggleywiggley, tiddle-de-wink, achoo!
Ridiculous words and phrases that
        keep you from feeling blue.
There's flibberty-gibbbet and alakazam, mares-eat-oats and
        thank you ma'am, razzmatazz and all that jazz
            and bibbity-bobbity   BOO!

There's ishkabibble and dibble-de dribble and snicklefritz
        and bug-in-a-rug, bump on a log and jiggedy-jog.
            gimme a hippomapatomus hug - mapotamus hug
                mapotamus hu-u-u-u-g ....
'Cause this is a (pause—beat, beat)
W a l k i n g   S o n g (spoken slowly)

2/21/87

Peace in Your Heart

Peace in your heart, let there be peace in your heart,
Let's find the place in each other to live, to love in peace.

Ease in your soul, let me just ease in your soul
Feeling the ease of your being with me with you,   communion.

Put your fears on my shoulder, lay your cares in my hand,
Weep your tears into my eyes and sew your spirit in my land.

Peace in your heart, let there be peace in your heart,
Let's find the place in each other to live, to love in peace.

Kiss your laughter to my lips, press your joy to my smile,
Lay your hopes next to my dreams and abide there awhile.

Ease in your soul, let me just ease in your soul,
Feeling the ease of your being with me with you,   communion.

Let me be your comfort. Can you be my harbor, my home?
Weaving the trail of the journey, we travel together, alone.

Peace in your heart, let me just ease in your soul,
Let's find the place in each other, just you, just me,
        communion,
Peace, communion.

For Fred, July 1985

The Tubby Song

(sung to the Bonanza TV show theme song)

I'm gonna, I'm gonna, I'm gonna take a tubby
I'm gonna, I'm gonna, I'm gonna take,
  gonna take a tubby now.
Rub a dub in the tub cleaning up my bod.
Soap 'n' stuff in the buff, gonna get clean, by God.

I'm gonna, I'm gonna, I'm gonna take a tubby
I'm gonna, I'm gonna, I'm gonna take,
  gonna take a tubby now.
Gonna get bare, shampoo my hair, fresh and sparkling clean.
Chase that dirt with a squirt, lather in between.

I'm gonna, I'm gonna, I'm gonna take a tubby
I'm gonna, I'm gonna, I'm gonna take,
  gonna take a tubby now.
Give three cheers, gonna wash my ears,
  gonna make 'em shine.
They'll get so clean that when they're seen
  you won't believe they're mine.

I'm gonna, I'm gonna, I'm gonna take a tubby
I'm gonna, I'm gonna, I'm gonna take,
  gonna take a tubby now.

For Ariel 1974?

The Hippopotamus Song

The hippopotamus, the hippopotamus,
        the hippopotamus who came to visit us.
He came upon a bus the hippopotamus,
        the hippopotamus who came to visit us.
Now, don't make a fuss 'bout the hippopotamus,
        he's very shy, I don't know why he's such a
                gloomy Gus.   BUT
Don't make a fuss
        a-bout the hippopotamus, the hippopota,
                hippopota, hippopotamus, yus!
For Ariel, 1974?

This poem is almost a postscript having been written most
recently. It is a never-ending call from the heart.

Simply a Touch

Touch me with your right hand of Love.
Touch me with your left hand of Mercy.
Hold me with your arms of Compassion.
Sing to me the songs of Joy.
Lift me up on the winds of Felicity.
I am yours.
Teach me.
August 30, 2022

Pax

He is here, a present shining star in this family's
      elysian field.
Tangible, no longer ethereal - warm, soft, strong, alive,
      vibrant being - this babe, this priceless piece of
        peace in our land.
We welcome, we embrace and surrender to his fresh
      promise.
We are humbled by our own child-like wonderment.
Birth, natural, yet always miraculous,
      Oh so very miraculous,
Originating joy and hope in this surprisingly small   package.
Ah these words, pathetically try to express it all!
I sit in truly wordless delight.
Time, now, for silence.

                November 29, 2022

The Gift

Raise the hands of my heart to the skies of
      Thine existence.
Spring my soul from magnetic earth with
      joy and exultation.
Infuse my words with comfort and kindness.
Strengthen my voice to pierce the barriers
      of selfishness and breach walls of separation.
Mark my course with divine direction that it may
      lead me to peace.
May I be a gift of harmony wrapped in soft swaddling.

                November 18, 2022

Pharoah, from the Track

There he lies sleeping, softly woofing, chasing some
      dream critter.
Thank Dog, it's not a metal rail rabbit.
Imagine a great expanse of field, the sun is shining,
      the breeze is light.
He's tucked his ears back, tightly to his head.
Pure aerodynamics!
Great powerful haunches rippling, great leaping
      strides propelling him onward.
Then circling back to his buddy, Shanti, bouncing
      'round her, four points off the ground.
"Romp, romp, romp with me."
She's not so fast, but accommodates his invitation.
And they cavort in canine delight. Then...
      no return to a second story crate, no rough hands,
        no harsh voices, just awakening on the soft
          carpet in the living room – because
            he is free, because he is ours.
Sometimes he makes his loving known as he bumps
      his head against my butt.
He rubs his long snout along my thigh.
It says, "I put my scent on you, I claim you."
Sometimes he stands, stoically accepting strokes and
      brushing, his great brown eyes, soft and almost
        enigmatic, speaking volumes.
Yes, this is as Dog intended.

August 20, 2014

Not yet do I stop

More haikus await their birth

Spirit progeny